THE TENTH ISLAND

THE TENTH ISLAND

DIANA MARCUM

Little a

Published by Little A, New York

www.apub.com

ISBN-13: 9781503941328 (hardcover)
ISBN-10: 1503941329 (hardcover)
ISBN-13: 9781503941311 (paperback)
ISBN-10: 1503941310 (paperback)

Cover Illustration by Rebecca Mock

Cover design by Faceout Studio, Spencer Fuller

Printed in the United States of America

First edition

For Bev and Mark

"Caught in between all you wish for and all you seen."

—*Joseph Arthur,* "In the Sun"

AUTHOR'S NOTE

There really is an Atlantic island where every summer, bulls run down the main streets and everyone has relatives visiting from California. Murphy (his real name) really ate those things. Moody (not his real name) really did break out in a cold sweat. The volcanoes, the history, the stories, the natural wonders, and the improbable coincidences in this book are true. Even though even now, I have a hard time believing it.

At home, in California, there is a box full of reporter's notebooks, dutifully filled with last names, ages, and direct quotes.

But I didn't use them much.

Somewhere along the line, my intention of writing a journalistic book on the Azorean diaspora took a detour. So, despite my job as a journalist, this is not a work of journalism, exactly.

Conversations are from my memory and my point of view. I used first names or nicknames or changed names entirely, as well as some identifying details. Because even though everyone knew I was a writer, many of the people in the book had no reason to believe I would write about *them*.

This is in no way a definitive report on the ties between the Azores and California. But it is a most affectionate one.

Diana Marcum

PART ONE

A Barn Party

It seems impossible now, like trying to remember when I couldn't read or didn't have a scar on my shin from that time I toppled off a bicycle, but I had never heard of the Azorean Islands when a photographer at the *Fresno Bee* dropped a picture on my desk of a man plowing a field with two oxen.

In California. In the twenty-first century.

The man stood on a flat cart. He had a cell phone to his ear. He was gesturing wildly with the other arm as great clouds of dust swirled behind him.

"I love this picture. I took it driving past," the photographer said. "Do you think you could find a story?"

"Absolutely," I told her. How could there not be a story there?

A couple of weeks later, I was on my way to the plower's house for an interview. I drove to a ranch in Tulare County, a part of California where everything is big. Big trucks, big belt buckles, big dairies, big silos and tractors and loading docks. This was before the big drought in California, and even the unplanted fields were spring green. I could see the snowcapped Sierra Nevada. Later, when the snow went missing, I wished that I had looked at it harder. For a while, it seemed gone forever, and I wanted to be sure the memory would hold.

No one was home, so I stretched out on the lawn near a white ranch fence. Above me there was a wide swath of sky with shape-shifting clouds. Say what you will about the hot, flat valley in the middle of California the rest of the year—but in April, after some good rains, I don't think you could find yourself lying in a prettier spot than in grass so green that you can't be sure whether the sky is really that blue or just looks brighter next to the blade you're twirling in front of your face.

It had been a tumultuous week, and it occurred to me that in all levels of crisis, it is a good idea to lie down outside and look up.

A truck pulled into the gravel driveway. The driver got out and introduced himself with wild arm waving, so I knew I had the right guy.

He was Morais, a wiry, exuberant Portuguese immigrant. If anyone has ever spoken in capital letters and exclamation points, it was Morais. The oxen were Amante and Brilliante. They shared a marked resemblance, both red Holsteins with white stars on their foreheads. They weren't yet full grown—at two years old, they were oxen teenagers, weighing, respectively, 1,940 and 1,860 pounds. Morais could tell them in Portuguese to turn right, turn left, and they did. He played Portuguese radio for them at night so they wouldn't get lonely.

I asked Morais to follow his usual routine while I watched. *"Vem para cá"*—"Come here to me," he called to the oxen in Portuguese, and they came over. He heaved up a wooden yoke carved by one of his cousins and slipped it over them. He hooked that to a 1,300-pound platform set on six earth-cutting metal discs.

He held a stick high in front of him and marched off like a drum major, his bulls falling in step behind him. He hadn't trained them by hitting them with the stick or bribing them with food. Since they were calves, he had walked them, teaching them right, left, and stop, using the stick as a visual cue.

"These animals is so smart, you cannot believe it! And they love me. These bulls *love* me. If I'm ready to go, they're ready to follow," he said.

Amante gave him a lick, as if to back up the claim.

Morais walked his field, stick in the air. The bulls dragged the discs behind him, kicking up clouds of dust that settled to reveal deep furrows. The sun glowed orange. Man, beasts, and swirling earth looked like a Depression-era work-project mural celebrating a lost farming past.

After a while, Morais stopped, ran to an ice chest, grabbed a beer, popped it open, and hopped on top of the platform to finish plowing.

He used his stick to tap brass tips that protected the oxen's horns. "*Levantem a cabeça*"—"Lift up your head," he told them, and they did.

His walkie-talkie phone rang, and Morais rode behind the bulls, carrying on a business conversation and juggling a bottle of beer, a phone, and two oxen. Someone drove by in a pickup, and Morais waved with the hand holding the phone.

Morais and the bulls took three hours to plow what would take forty-five minutes with a tractor. That included a break to give the bulls a rest while he sipped another cold beer.

"This is a lot harder. This is work. But I'm more happy with my bulls, believe me, than I would be with a tractor," he told me.

When he finished for the day, he leaped off the platform like a gymnast landing a jump with arms stretched overhead.

"*This* is my life!" he shouted.

He said that in the mornings he hauled cattle for a living and made good money doing it. He could afford a tractor. But the oxen were his tie to "the old country" he had left as a teenager—the Azores, nine Portuguese specks of land surrounded by the Atlantic Ocean for at least nine hundred miles in every direction. So he plowed the way they had during his childhood on the islands and, according to him, the way they still plowed there today.

He pulled a battered red photo album from his truck's glove compartment and showed me pictures of green Azorean fields divided by hedges of lilac-colored hydrangeas. He showed me waves crashing against black volcanic rock and his ancient stone house next to the sea, the home where he returned every summer.

"Over there the air is so clean, so nice. The ocean is right there. The fish are fresh, you catch and eat them, and the potatoes are so good, you won't believe it.

"We make wine. Put on shorts and get in there and smash grapes, and when you drink right away is sweet like juice. Every year when we get back from there, we're fat," Morais said.

He loved his island house in the Azores so much that at the end of each summer, when he left, he had to have someone else close the door for him.

"I'm a guy that came from the old country. I never go to school five minutes in this country, and still I work and I do good. I *love* my money. God bless this country," he said.

"But when I leave to close my door over there, I cry like a baby. I try so hard not to, but I cry."

He told me he was throwing a party the next weekend and that if I wanted to see a piece of the Azores, I should come and bring friends. I couldn't use the experience for my article; it would have run by then. I didn't care. I wanted to see that party.

My next-door neighbor Donald, the paper's arts and culture writer, was more into Broadway than bulls. But that Saturday, I rounded him up with my boyfriend, Das, a tall, shy designer who read books on the evolution of coat hanger shapes. Together we stepped out of my little Toyota and onto a ranch filled with supersized white pickup trucks. The tail end of a parade came down the road—oxen with flower-decorated harnesses and a band of guitar players. Morais had no need for road closures or permits; everyone for about two hundred miles was some relation such as "my son's fiancée is niece to his brother." Who would complain?

Near the barn, a group of men were cheering on a "bull pull," which is exactly what it sounds like—two bulls pulling in opposite directions, a bovine tug-of-war.

Then some of the younger guys, who owned pickup trucks that cost about as much as a country tract home, started trash-talking one another's RPMs. Next thing we knew, it was the hell with the bulls, hook up the trucks. Tires screamed. People cheered.

We were handed plastic cups constantly refilled with ice-cold Budweiser. After a few more emptied kegs, the yokes that had been worn by steers were placed on men. They took off their shirts, put on the chains, and strained against one another with all their might.

Duo after duo pulled against each other in the mud until they collapsed. Donald and I were somewhat loath to turn our attention from the sweaty men. Even Das seemed transfixed, if not for exactly the same reasons.

But a group of older women, giggling and wearing drab, shapeless black dresses, encircled us. They waved one of the younger guys in the bull-pull audience over to translate. Which one of these men was my husband, they wanted to know, several of them wagging fingers between my gay friend and metrosexual beau. I told them they were both my boyfriends, and they laughed.

I asked the young man why the women were all dressed in black. He said they were widows but that the most recently bereaved had lost her husband twenty years ago and she hadn't liked him anyway. I asked our bull-pull translator which one of the widows had the most boyfriends. They laughed, and all pointed to the woman who was by far the oldest.

I looked around in vain trying to find one sign that I was still in California. I got the feeling that I was in an Azorean Brigadoon—a village out of place and time. All the conversations and exclamations swirling around us were in Portuguese. That night, after a hearty meal of *sopas* ladled out of huge pots and *linguiça* and Portuguese breads and cheeses, the party moved into the barn for dancing. The walls were hung with tablecloths showing the nine Azorean Islands. My first look at a map of the place that would come to have such a hold on me was on picnic linens.

Morais's island was São Jorge, a long, thin oblong in the center of the map tablecloth floating between a pineapple, a windmill, and a whale. The last dance of the night in the candlelit barn was the *chamarita*—folk dance—of his island. The party's mood changed. The music was slow and dark. The dancers took one step, two steps. They stopped and clapped their hands twice. It was more of a rite than a dance.

Morais was teary-eyed when he returned to us from dancing with a childhood friend. All the dancers seemed choked up.

I was chatting with an earnest teen who was telling me of her devotion to Azorean folk dance. I asked her why the dancers were crying.

"I think for the old ones, it's because they are remembering," she said. "And everyone else is longing for something that we don't even know what it is anymore."

I couldn't stop thinking about that night. I kept wondering about those islands smack-dab in the middle of the Atlantic. When I stopped to consider it, I realized I had always had a thing for islands. In my twenties, trapped as a cocktail waitress / bookstore clerk living in an apartment where cockroaches dived for cover when I switched on the kitchen light, I had kept a poster of the Greek isles on my wall. Whitewashed walls against a blue stretching sea. Islands tend to be the go-to symbol for escape. Or maybe for me, it was more the feeling that I *was* an island, separate and alone.

I read up and found the Azores near the top of a *National Geographic* list of unspoiled island destinations in the world. It gave them points for being "authentic and likely to remain so."

They are protected by their lack of the basic necessities for seaside tourism: resorts, white-sand beaches, and consistently warm weather. The saying goes that the Azores have four seasons—every day.

Even in ancient times, they were off the beaten path. They seem to appear on old maps of the world, then disappear again for hundreds of years, lost to fog and currents and the vagaries of the sea. Over the centuries, they were rumored to be the remnants of the lost continent of Atlantis or the last kingdom of the Lusiads, founded by Lusus, the son of Bacchus, the god of wine. Some Azoreans told me they believe their ancestors to be disgraced Portuguese nobles and bastard sons. Others thought the original inhabitants were peasants shipped from the mainland against their will to colonize. Recent archaeology finds suggest there may have been even earlier, unknown inhabitants who disappeared before the Portuguese arrived, raising the question of how people got to the middle of the ocean before the known advent of sailing ships.

Myths cling to the Azores like mist to their volcanic peaks. It's a place where people speak of chatting to someone who died fifty years ago as if they were visiting with a neighbor down the street. Even modern discoveries are cast in otherworldly terms: when Europe's rarest orchid was found atop a volcanic ridge in Pico in 2013, botanist Richard Bateman of Kew Gardens in London said researchers described it as a "Lost World."

Mark Twain mentioned the Azores in *The Innocents Abroad* but only to say, "Out of our whole ship's company there was not a solitary individual who knew anything whatever about them."

The islands once exported oranges to England, but the Azores' main export has always been its people. About a million people born in the Azores and their descendants live in North America—four times more than the nine islands' population. During the latest wave of mass migration, between 1958 and 1980, more than one-third of the Azores' population left, running from a volcano's eruption, poverty, and a Portuguese dictator. Many of these people came from the island of Terceira (pronounced "ter-sey-rah") and settled in California's rural Central Valley, cows being the common denominator. In both places, Azoreans owned and worked on dairies.

The Azoreans who emigrated were homesick. Actually, it reached beyond that. There is a Portuguese word, *saudade*, that they say has no translation. It's bigger than homesickness or missing someone. It's a yearning that can be expressed in no other language. It is, as one Azorean friend puts it, "a strictly Portuguese word."

They say it has something to do with death but mostly life and maybe the ocean and probably time, and the only way to understand *saudade* is to listen to fado, the Portuguese art of the sad song. Or, more accurately, songs of longing.

So in California—as they had earlier around Boston and Toronto—displaced Azoreans filled with *saudade* re-created island life as best they could. In isolated farm towns, they staged fado concerts with only the old songs and festivals that religiously followed custom. Even their language is a throwback, peppered with expressions of forty years ago.

Each summer, planeloads of Azoreans return to the islands. They stay in their family homes. They revisit old loves and feuds and family ties, and there is a culture clash between the New World and the Old World—with the Old World visiting from California.

For several summers, I had driven through miles of hot Central Valley landscapes with more cows than people. Mysteriously empty diners. Trucks that stayed parked in the same spot for months. I had also, for many years, longed for things swallowed in the past, forever out of reach. Now I finally knew where everyone went. And I may have found a word for something inside me that I didn't even know what it was anymore.

Saudade.

A Low Point

The day before I visited Morais's ranch for the first time, I was lying motionless on a couch in Fresno.

I had piled every blanket in my house on top of me, translating the weight of my stalled career into a suffocating pile of wool and fleece and a puffy throw quilt. Looking back, I should have suspected I was about to bump into something like, say, a rumored lost Atlantis. Stories almost always begin with a person at their low point.

Earlier that week, in a fit of, in my opinion, righteous anger, I had slammed a draft of an article down on the desk of a top editor at the paper where I was a reporter and walked out of the office and the building, maybe (I told myself) for good.

Now, I know that people with tempers tend to be slyly proud of the trait. Even exaggerate their outbursts. To my mild disappointment, this isn't me. I'm not decisive enough to throw things, always seeing 1,372 sides to each conundrum. It is no wonder that all my sweaters are gray. A work mentor once coached me on how not to smile too much during meetings (or "not gape like a deranged idiot" in her terms).

So after the blowup, I was not glorying in some fiery tempestuous nature—I was sinking like a drunk on a feather bed. There was a knock at the door that I ignored. My down-the-street neighbor and colleague, Jack Moody, kept tapping until I finally crawled out from under my bedcovers and let him in. I always called him Moody; I felt his last name aptly described his temperament. No one had to coach him to not smile too much.

He was the photographer on the ill-fated project at the center of the fight. Together we had haunted a meth-fueled town in a barren stretch of California's Central Valley. "Welcome to Hell" was spray-painted on the town population sign. We tagged along with three women in a U-Haul as they moved back to Arkansas, where their families had come from during the Great Depression. It was a reverse Dust Bowl migration, and we followed Route 66 to smoke-filled Denny's restaurants and Super 8 motels and towns where fried fish is the standard breakfast. Moody thought the most surprising part of our road trip was that in the car, I didn't talk as much or as fast as he was afraid I would. I, on the other hand, was pleased to discover that he talked at all.

The fiasco was sort of Moody's fault. He'd had me look at the captions that went with his photographs for the newspaper series. I told him to change one that said a woman named Brownie was a resident of the town of Alpaugh. She was born in Alpaugh; she had lived most of her life in Alpaugh; her family was in Alpaugh. But at the time she decided to go east, she was living with her boyfriend in the nearby town of Riverdale. Moody forgot, and I circled it on the galleys with a fat red pen because I wanted everything perfect.

This was about when the *New York Times* discovered one of its reporters had been fabricating stories, even pretending he had gone places he hadn't. Editors everywhere were tense and on guard.

My managing editor thought my changing the photo caption meant I had made up Brownie's Alpaugh connection and that she had caught her very own rogue reporter. I pointed out that I was the one wielding the red pen—not exactly sneaky—but I was shouted down. The project's editor knew the ins and outs of Brownie's living arrangements, but he'd had his own fight with the higher-ups the month before and had picked up his family and made his own reverse migration to Florida. I was on my own.

The managing editor, head held high, said they were going to hold the story and check every word.

"Have at it," I yelled, for once knowing what trembling rage felt like (a bit nauseating).

Thank God for Moody. He was there for every reported conversation. Most of the time he wasn't listening. He had a way of disconnecting from everything verbal and turning his entire being into a camera. But his photos would back me up by documenting everyone as real. Short of some bonehead mistake on my part, I would be all right. But I had seldom written any story where I didn't startle awake at night, fearing I had made that bonehead mistake, and this was worse.

I told Moody that the story we'd spent two months reporting was on indefinite hold.

"Oh well, it'll run eventually," he said with a shrug. He was the worst. I tell him management is attacking my credibility, and his answer to this treachery is "Oh well"?

I felt the first stirrings of resolve. To fix my life. To, maybe even, perhaps, at some point, get off the couch. I had to get out of this place or I'd turn into Moody—no lifeblood. A shoulder shrugger.

"Why is your hair so dark?" he asked.

"I haven't taken a shower in a couple of days," I admitted. "I would have had to leave the couch."

"So that's grease?" he asked, clearly fascinated.

"Yes," I said.

"Is that fuzzy thing you're wearing what they call a bathrobe?" he asked.

"Yes," I said.

"You look terrible," he said.

Moody wasn't the type for a consoling hug. He awkwardly patted the blankets somewhere in the vicinity of my feet.

"OK, then, Marcum, take care," he said as he left. "You might want to try peeling off a blanket or two."

After he was gone, I went back to staring at the stripes on the wall that the afternoon sun made coming through the window blinds. I made a note that should I ever have a mental breakdown, my version would be catatonic.

The weird part was that I had genuine heartache in my past, so you would think I'd be inoculated against mere office intrigue, not sprawl on a couch. But it doesn't work like that.

I have these theories of life: the Canopy Bed Theory, the Day of Haircut Theory. (The latter is actually my friend Shellee's theory, but I subscribe. It is alternatively known as the Best Weather on the Last Day of Vacation Theory.) I find it comforting to codify and title life's phenomena. I had come up with one of my earliest theories—the Paper-Cut Theory—after my parents died, when I was a teenager, to explain to myself how anything could get to me after living through that.

The Paper-Cut Theory

> This theory holds that the tiny cuts made by bad bosses, broken romances, and the like sting more than real grief. It's the difference between a deep throbbing wound and a paper cut. Our fingers have more nerves near the surface because that's how we explore the world. So it hurts like hell when paper slices us. At the same time, scientists believe that our bodies know it's not really life-threatening, so all the natural protective mechanisms, such as endorphins and bleeding, don't kick into gear. And since paper is microscopically ragged, it leaves a jagged cut. Unlike the clean slice of a razor, which can kill us.

My father, Wilbur Ira, who understandably went by Mark, was a steelworker and a mechanic from Kentucky with a fourth-grade education. Tall for his age, he stole one of his older brothers' birth certificates and joined the army when he was fourteen years old to get out of poverty that he said was deeper than pig shit and stickier than molasses. He never entirely escaped. He said poor ran in our family. He'd been wounded during the Korean War. When my mother got mad at him, she pulled out his Purple Heart. She said it reminded her that little things don't matter.

My dad had a saying for everything. I knew which one he'd pull out in this case: "There's a cheap version of everything." Meaning, don't get fooled by the fake stuff.

So was this really about survival—a worry that I'd lose my job? No. I was a reporter at a midsize regional paper. I'd made more money as a cocktail waitress, and I could again if I had to. But it was a bit more than a paper-cut fight with the boss: I was failing at the only things I thought I was good at, writing and maintaining an unwarranted sense of optimism.

When you are the child of parents who sacrificed and strived but were squashed by the world at every turn and then died young, you are supposed to be the thing that makes it somehow all make sense, to make their lives mean something.

And I was lying on the couch with dirty hair, dreading the next day. My fantasy of myself as special was taking a serious beating.

I tried to rally by turning to every childish gambit in the book. I would get through this. Why, *those* people were not the boss of *me*. OK, technically they were. But I would speak to them only when spoken to, like a sullen teenager. I would concentrate on writing little stories that were unlikely to draw anyone else's attention but simply appealed to me. (Not that I am recommending pouty withdrawal as a general career strategy.)

I had gone to elementary school during a time of experimental education in California. We listened to books on tape and carved soap, and our teacher Pam brought in her guitar and taught us songs to lean on in times of what she called emotional distress. With a nod to Pam, I turned up the volume on her standby, an old Simon and Garfunkel song: "I am a rock. I am an island . . . and an island never cries."

Then I got off the couch, washed my hair, drove to California dairy country where I met Morais, and began to dream of visiting an island instead of being one.

Capelinhos

Growing up in California, you learn early that living amid great beauty comes with great risk. Our sunlit mountains, fertile valleys, and sparkling coastal cities are vulnerable to fires, floods, and earthquakes. Try finding someone in California who has never been evacuated. The volcanic Azores are also no strangers to natural disasters. The ties between the islands and the United States are made of lava.

On September 16, 1957, there was a series of very small earthquakes off the coast of Faial. No one paid much attention. On September 27, a spotter manning one of the *vigias*—whale lookouts—saw turbulent water and signaled that a school of whales had been spotted.

It wasn't whales.

The water became agitated, as if it were boiling. The lighthouse keepers and the sailors in port at Capelinhos fled. About a half mile out in the ocean, a giant white fountain spouted. Three days later, it looked like an atomic mushroom cloud. Steam and black ash billowed 4,200 feet in the air. For a month there was the sound of booming explosions as well as spooky clouds of steam and mud.

A new island, three hundred feet tall, rose from the sea. Three reporters rowed out to the rumbling land, and one—in a nonjournalistic show of nationalism—planted a Portuguese flag.

For months ash fell in drifts so heavy, they broke tile roofs, covering fields and killing Faial's crops. People walked around with umbrellas to shield themselves from the black rain. The volcano dust formed an isthmus connecting the volcano and Faial, and clouds of it blocked the sun, putting the entire archipelago under darkened skies.

On the night of May 12, more than 450 earthquakes shook Faial. Churches were packed. On one cliff, women wearing the traditional *capas*—hooded black capes from an earlier century—watched the sea and wailed. Some threw rosary beads into the ocean as offerings. Many people didn't expect to live through the night. But no one died.

Two days after the shaking, lava shot into the sky. They heard the explosions on Flores Island, 126 miles away. By August, the cone was five hundred feet high and Faial was almost a square mile bigger than it had been before. That October, the volcano "fell asleep," and its nap has been undisturbed since—although volcanologists still list it as active.

The eruption turned out to be a lot of people's tickets to America.

Azoreans had been part of the United States from the beginning. Peter Francisco, sometimes called the Portuguese Paul Bunyan for his size and strength, was said to have fought in the American Revolution, and myth has it that he carried a cannon out of enemy reach on top of his shoulder. John Philip Sousa wrote "The Stars and Stripes Forever" aboard a steam freighter traveling from Terceira to the United States, combining forever the Azorean love of marching bands and American history. By the 1920s there were thriving, well-established Azorean American communities and a steady stream of newcomers.

America has long been divided between those who believe its strength lies in diversity and those who are afraid of outsiders and blame social ills on whoever is in the latest wave of migrants.

In the mid-1800s, the anti-immigration Know Nothing Party rode a backlash against Irish and German immigrants and painted Catholicism as undermining American values. In the 1920s the resentments were focused on immigrants from southern and eastern European countries. A series of laws were passed aimed at keeping out poor and uneducated people. Immigration from the Azores fell dramatically.

By the 1950s, a hundred years after that, the poem on the base of the Statue of Liberty still found little voice in law. Those words—"Give me your tired, your poor, / Your huddled masses yearning to breathe free"—were written by Emma Lazarus, an American poet who came from a refugee Jewish Portuguese family. Even during the harshest days of a fascist regime in Portugal, when intellectuals and artists were being kidnapped and tortured and people were starving, the yearly quota for Portuguese immigrants was 503 people.

Then Capelinhos erupted.

Lawmakers with a lot of Portuguese voters in their districts, including the then senator John F. Kennedy, pushed to let thousands of Azoreans into the United States under the Azorean Refugee Acts of 1958 and 1960. Immigration reform in 1965 opened the door to more immigrants and made getting a visa easier for people with family in the United States.

In the Azores, there was still widespread poverty, and families were desperate to leave before their sons were old enough to be drafted to fight in Angola and other colonial wars.

This was the origin story of the communities I had encountered in Central California, most of whom had arrived during the seventies.

A more current tie was that of a Portuguese plane that left Oakland International Airport every Monday between May and September bound for Terceira, the island with the most connections to the Central Valley. The plane was always packed. There was a return flight every Wednesday.

I pitched a story about the scene at the airport during this homeland exodus, and the paper agreed (need of a paycheck had kept me in the fold), and now I was seated in a big black SUV with Frank Serpa, his wife, Fernanda, and their handyman, Joe, who was driving. On late-night local TV commercials, Frank was "Serpaman," a superhero who could fly through the air, cape flapping, to bring you a good deal at one of his car lots. Frank showed me videos of him getting chased by bulls, his reason for going back to the Azores every summer.

"Look! Look! That bull kicked my butt all the way into the kitchen!" he narrated, as sure enough, on-screen Frank jumped a wall and ran into a house, followed by a bull that jumped the wall as well. "It's a way to feel like a young man!" said Frank.

From the front seat, Fernanda turned around and winked at me.

What Frank was showing me was *tourada à corda*—bull on a rope. These bullfights are not like the Spanish type, in which the bull is killed and the danger is enclosed in a ring. In Terceira, a bull of an ancient strain, bred to be aggressive, is let loose on the main street in town. Well, almost loose. Seven shepherds—*pastores*—in white shirts with puffy sleeves and flat, black hats hold a rope attached to the bull.

If the bull decides to run full force ahead, the dashingly attired men on the other end of the rope are simply along for the ride, as I would later witness. They skid through town on a bovine-powered tow. More often the bull goes to the side or runs back toward his handlers, in which case the rope is slack and of no immediate use, and a common danger to spectators is getting knocked over by an agile shepherd leaping a wall in a single bound to escape.

The saying goes, *"A primeira pancada é sempre do touro"*—"The first strike belongs to the bull." Sometimes, if all seven men work perfectly in conjunction and the rope isn't too tangled up, they can pull a bull off a victim by the third or fourth hit. Not that the shepherds are there to protect people. They are there to take care of the bull, herding the valuable star of the show back into the crate at the end of the fight.

All summer long, every night, somewhere on the island there is a rope bullfight. Sometimes three on the same night. No self-respecting village will go the summer without hosting its own night of havoc. Families nail flimsy plywood over the walls that separate their colorfully trimmed houses from the street. On the night of the event, there are food trucks selling beers and *bifanas*—spicy pork cutlet and slow-cooked onions on a flour-dusted bun. Groups of people hang out of every window, every doorway. Street vendors hawk candy. Girls sit on walls and flirt with boys in the street below. Men wave their bottles of Portuguese beer and endless cigarettes in concert with conversational points. Children pretend to be bulls, charging one another. There is always, somewhere, the sound of a marching band warming up.

Then a *foguetes*, a flaming skyrocket, whistles through the air with a fiery swish and—*boom!*—leaves a smudge of black on the sky. That's the warning: get out of the street, go behind the walls, climb a tree, or face a bull.

The crate that holds the bull is already rocking before they open the door. Another screeching fiery skyrocket and—*boom!*—the bull is in the street.

Most of the men who stay in the street (and it is almost always men) run away as soon as the bull so much as glances in their direction. A few others "play with the bull." They taunt him with umbrellas and call him with flapping dish towels. A real crowd-pleaser is a man who can touch the bull's horns and then run with his parasol in a circle with the bull close by, without getting gored. These self-styled matadors are in sneakers or flip-flops.

Often the bull's attention will wander, and he'll charge the houses, knocking into the flimsy plywood. Sometimes the bull will plunge his horns into the church doors or jump a wall, and grandmas and grandpas will tumble off their lawn chairs. Parents toss their kids like footballs—excuse me, *bolas de futebol*—away from a bull. This is when it's considered a really good bullfight.

Speeding down Highway 99, on the way to the airport, before I had seen any of this for myself, Frank showed me a book that explained that the fights created "situations dramatic and comical to arouse the passions of the people." The same book explained that the origins of the tradition, dating back to at least the early 1600s, are specific to Terceira alone. "Canna you believe it?" asked Frank, seeming astonished that the custom of getting together to have a bull rampage through town had not taken the globe by storm.

I was not immediately seeing the charm.

"What do you think is exactly the appeal to people like yourself?" I asked Frank while we drove to the airport.

But this is where it became Fernanda's story. "It's a 'cause of the way we drove out Spain!" she said, eyes flashing and, like Frank, adding connecting syllables to English that made it roll like Portuguese as she recounted the tale.

Once, back in the summer of 1581, all of Portugal except Terceira had come under the control of the Spanish Crown. The Spanish king sent ten ships and more than one thousand soldiers to invade the island. (History books confirm that much. Some say the next part is romanticized legend. But with the passionate way Fernanda told the story, I couldn't help believing every word. Especially since history has a way of not crediting women.)

In Fernanda's telling, on that fateful day of the Battle of Salga, the Spanish troops found only a few soldiers defending the bay. They moved in, burning fields and houses. They wounded and captured the husband and son of Brianda Pereira, a beautiful noblewoman. Brianda made a plan: The Terceirans kept their bulls, a special breed known to be fierce and aggressive, in the center of the island in a caldera—the valley formed by the collapsed mouth of the volcano. Brianda exhorted the women of the island to drive the bulls from the caldera and onto the beach to attack the Spanish soldiers. Farmers followed behind with pitchforks and any weapons they could find. The Spanish were terrorized by the beasts. They fled back to their ships.

And that, said Fernanda, is why to this day Terceira men love the bulls. "But I do notta like it," she said. "Frank's agonna get himself killed."

It was not an empty worry. Deaths are, surprisingly, relatively rare. But every year people get injured, and there have been fatalities.

When we arrived at the Oakland airport, it seemed no one in the SunTrips Budget Tours line had ever heard of packing light. People carried bulky presents for relatives in the Azores. And everyone in line had relatives in the Azores. One woman carried a box of live chickens. Frank bumped into a Tulare dairyman he'd grown up with in Terceira. They told me about how they used to make cars out of corncobs because they had no toys. And they would steal fruit because they were hungry. It sounded a lot like how my mother described growing up poor in Colorado.

Frank immigrated when he was twenty-four. He arrived at Fresno Airport in 1971 with one dollar and one penny in his pocket. He bought a 3 Musketeers bar, leaving him with seventy-six cents, which he still keeps in a safe as a reminder of where he started. His original plan had been to make money and return to his island, but now, at fifty-eight, he had American children and grandchildren, and Frank had changed too.

"Let's put it this way," Joe told me in the car. "On all the computers at work, Frank keeps signs that say, 'Don't leave for tomorrow what you can do today.' And the Azores way is 'If you can do it today, you can do it tomorrow. Why not tomorrow?'"

A couple of years earlier, the men working on a remodel of the Serpas' Terceira house had started packing up after a few hours to go to a street bullfight. Frank said, "Hey! I'm the guy paying you. What's more important: the guy paying you or the bullfight?"

They said, "The bullfight," and left.

"Shoulda heard him," Fernanda said, laughing. "He was so mad. He was saying, 'I can't take these people! I'm going to leave.'"

Fernanda asked me why I wanted to write a story for the newspaper about Azoreans going back to the islands. I told her the truth: it was just an excuse so I could learn more about the Azores. I was becoming obsessed with them.

"You should have your paper send you to Terceira," Frank said.

I told him that was like suggesting the local coffee shop send a waitress to Milan to further explore coffee making.

"Wella, then, justa go yourself. You know? Write a movie, something like that," he said.

About a week later, I was in my backyard, planning no immediate European jaunts, when my phone rang, showing Frank's number. I added the seven hours ahead. He was calling me at four in the morning island time. I could barely hear him over music and people laughing.

"Hey-a Diana," he said. "I'm-a here with my good, good friend. He owns a beautiful hotel, right next to the water. I tell him there's this writer who likes the Azores but never been to the Azores. He says, 'Tell her to come and stay at my hotel. No problem.' We got another friend way high with the airline. He'll get you a free ticket. No-a strings. We know you can't make-a no promises."

I thanked him but told him reporters weren't allowed to take free trips. And I didn't know anyone who might ask me for a movie script.

"Don't write anything," he said. "Fernanda says to tell you, you should say yes."

Fernanda got on the phone. She told me that the American way is that "you wash my back, I wash yours." But the Azorean way is that everybody works together to make enough for everybody. "These men put together a big pot of *sopa*—you grab a bowl."

The next day I was having lunch with a writer I considered a mentor even though we were only a few years apart. Even to his face, I called him the Manly Author. He had a lot in common with those Azorean bulls. Small spaces made him edgy; you could almost imagine him pawing the ground. He was a Very Serious Investigative Journalist for a big paper, and his favorite line of attack was the hard charge.

It was with a sense of embarrassment that I told him how tempted I was by Frank's offer for a free trip to the Azores. I figured my resolve needed the disapproval he was sure to provide.

"Go," he said. "You got no conflict. Just don't write anything else about them for the Fresno paper. You got one foot out the door anyway."

"But what do you think they expect? What do they want from me?" I asked.

"Same thing everyone wants," he said. "They want someone to know their story. And, shit, maybe it's supposed to be a part of *your own story*."

Somehow that seemed exactly what I was missing: my own story.

Come September, I was on a flight out of the valley and to Terceira—the potato-shaped island in the middle of the tablecloth. It was the last departing flight of the season, the only one that had an open seat left.

I struck up a conversation with Gladys, who sat across the aisle, by complimenting her colorful scarf. She started teaching me Portuguese words until her partner, Filomena, couldn't stand it any longer. "She's Cuban!" she cried. "You are learning Portuguese from the only other non-Portuguese person on this plane!"

Gladys had emigrated from Cuba to California with her mother when she was four years old. The only English either of them knew was "Coca-Cola, please." The young Gladys had been scared and didn't see how they were going to find their way from one place to another.

"Don't worry," her mother told her. "You can get to China just by asking."

The next morning, I watched the sun rise over the Atlantic Ocean, no land in sight.

When I finally saw the Azores, they were brilliant green specks in a dark sea, peeking in and out of mist. No wonder they may have been lost and found a few times. In the 1300s they seemed to appear on maps but not exactly in the right latitude or groupings. Maybe those islands were the Azores, or maybe they were just some of the mythical islands that often decorated ancient maps, along with dragons and sea monsters.

A couple of hundred years later, the Portuguese discovered—or possibly rediscovered—the Azores. The islands had been the first stop in the Age of Discovery. It had happened before. Maybe it would work for me too.

The Tenth Island

I was told about Alberto before I met him.

"He has seventy-eight years, but he looks the age of fifty. He has a big being," Frank told me when I was still in California.

José ("zhwa-zay" is the Portuguese pronunciation), Frank's cousin or nephew—I wasn't quite clear, but they are somehow related—and his wife, Luisa, picked me up at the airport and later in the week picked me up to go to Alberto and Dona Maria's for a traditional Portuguese meal cooked *o forno*—in a wood-burning oven.

"Alberto, you will love," said Luisa. She had a distinctly Portuguese beauty, with long-lashed green eyes that dipped down at the corners, a copper suntan, and gleaming black hair. I was pale and envious.

"Alberto has much intelligence. Like encyclopedia," said José, who had a computer in his basement that he had built from scraps. People came from all around to use José's Skype, which at the time was cutting-edge technology.

When we arrived, Dona Maria already had orange flames leaping out of the oven. It was in a kitchen separate from the house, back by a large garden. Long wooden paddles, in different shapes to take different kinds of bread out of the oven, hung on the walls. A wooden table that Alberto had made held an enormous bowl of fresh figs.

Before we had left for Alberto and Dona Maria's, Luisa had picked a basket of red and yellow tomatoes from her garden, arranging them just so in a basket. She placed them next to the figs. In the Azores, I was surrounded by still-life paintings come to life.

Alberto had a wide-open face and big fleshy palms that he waved as he talked. He immediately pressed a cold Sagres beer in my hand and walked me through their wild, bountiful garden. They were growing dill, guava trees, and potatoes, among other things.

"Look how much higher the plants are on this side," Alberto told me. "It's because we throw all the trash from the kitchen out in the garden, and we can't throw that far." I looked down and saw the eggshells and coffee grounds that made Alberto's garden grow higher on one side than on the other.

Their house had two stories and a velvet lawn that marked them as returning immigrants. (It would be explained to me later that on an island of green fields and hills, only Americans and Canadians felt the need to mow.) The grass unrolled down to the cottage kitchen; beyond that, the garden, and beyond that, the blue backdrop of the sea.

Alberto said rich Americans were always asking to buy the house. "You don't have enough money," he would tell them.

"Try me," they would say.

"You don't have enough money because it's not for sale," he'd answer.

"And you know, they kind of relax after that," he said. "They are relieved when they find there is something that's not for sale."

He bought the land, including the house across the street where Dona Maria was born and where their Canadian-born daughter now lived, for about $6,000 in the 1980s.

We walked down to the sea, picking our way across black volcanic rocks. Alberto picked up a handful of seashells. "Look, these animals, the ones who left their little homes behind, don't come from the waters anywhere around here. But their shells are on this island," he said. "The world is a small place, and the currents can carry anyone anywhere."

Alberto and Dona Maria lived twenty-five years in Canada, raising their children there. He had his guitar with him in Canada, but he said he never played it because he had no free time or friends who had free time to play music with him. I asked Alberto whether there was anything he loved from Canada, anything he'd brought back with him.

"My pension," he said.

We ate our meal cooked in the old wood-burning stone oven in the main house, which had a modern kitchen with a microwave and an ice maker. There was a big table groaning with food: *cozido à portuguesa*—every kind of meat, beef, pork, chicken, and various blood sausages, amazing potatoes from the garden, white potatoes that were as sweet as pastry, chewy yams, and creamy little round *batatas* as rich as butter. There was bread straight from the fire and pumpkins from the garden sliced in half and sprinkled with brown sugar and transformed into something intense by their stone-and-fire roasting. My favorite Portuguese word is the word for pumpkin—*abóbora*—it's just fun to say.

I said I didn't see how I was going to know when to stop, with so much food to be sampled.

"Follow me. Stop when I do," Alberto said.

He didn't stop for a long time. He drank at least a liter of red wine by himself and kept filling up my glass from another bottle. After dinner, which lasted hours, José and Alberto brought out their handmade *guitarras*. Alberto had made his first Portuguese guitar twenty years before he learned how to play it.

Alberto and José played and sang a few songs. I asked about Terceira's *chamarita*—its folk dance. I had seen it danced at *festas* in California.

"You know the *chamarita*?" Alberto asked.

"I've seen it, but I need to be reminded," I said.

Alberto danced me around, showing the steps. Then he sat back down to his guitar. "Show me your dancing," he said.

I had once taught children's dance classes, a career that ended ignobly. The unfortunate incident had come up earlier in conversation with José and Luisa. It was at Miss Martha Lee's School of Dance. Martha Lee was an old-school ballerina. She stood as straight as a pole and was just as slender. She wore her eternally jet-black hair pulled back in a bun. She had a toy poodle that she carried under one arm. Martha Lee's nail polish always matched a bow on the poodle's head, and sometimes the poodle had matching nail polish as well.

Martha Lee was no fan of jazz dance, but that was what the kids wanted, so she had begrudgingly added me, a mediocre-at-best dancer with minimal ballet training, to the roster.

I had one class of ten-year-olds, who were particularly klutzy even for ten-year-olds. On the day in question, we were going through a jazz warm-up, which involved isolating different body parts. The idea was that the whole class would move the same body part at the same time, keeping the beat. This was not happening. I kept trying slower and slower music until I settled on a thudding Prince song that even uncoordinated children could follow. We moved down from our heads to our ribs to isolating our hips, which involved thrusting out one hip to the far corner of the room, then the other hip in the other direction, and then swiveling our pelvises: right-center-left-center-and-*aroooooooound*.

It was at this moment, when I had the children grinding in what some may consider a stripper move, that Martha Lee popped in to observe and I suddenly registered the lyrics of "Darling Nikki," which has a woman in a hotel lobby practicing, shall we say, *self-care* behind a magazine.

I was fired on the spot.

When I told the story, with another friend translating, José and Luisa had laughed, and they had known the song. It wasn't just seashells that proved the world's interconnection. There was Prince.

I danced around the kitchen a bit as ordered.

"Yes, you dance well!" Alberto exclaimed, and I was inordinately pleased, feeling a bit of redemption from being a fired dance teacher.

José got up and danced with Luisa, playing his *guitarra* as he danced. Alberto and Dona Maria didn't dance together because they both agreed that they didn't move well together and that it made them cranky and argumentative to try. They each thought the other was a terrible dancer. They said this to each other's face with no reproach. We danced until we were flushed and breathless.

Then José and Alberto played more songs, eventually coming to fados—songs of great emotion. On one song, Luisa and Dona Maria sang along, and they all wept.

It was a song by Amalia Rodrigues, the Queen of Fado. I didn't know the song then, but later I would know it well. They say it's a tricky thing to translate fado. The words resist a different language. But a rough translation of "A Minha Canção é Saudade"—"My Song Is of Longing"—is:

> I cry my own nostalgia
> I weep in pity for myself
> I cry, absorbed in my own longing.

We talked late into the evening. Speaking about the Azorean communities in California, I called them the Tenth Island because that's what they called themselves. I said that at first I had thought it meant only California. But now I understood it was the entire diaspora, including the Boston area and Canada.

Alberto laughed. "You think the Tenth Island is a place or a group of people?" he scoffed. "The Tenth Island is what you carry inside you. It's what's left when everything else falls away. Those of us who live between worlds just know the Tenth Island better. No matter where I have lived—I have never left my island."

Later that night, I was back at the hotel in the ancient port city of Angra do Heroísmo. From the hotel I could see Mount Brasil. Its outline looked like a sphinx with its legs stretching out into the sea, guarding the city. There was a monument up there commemorating Angra's role in the Age of Discovery, something also marked throughout the city in the designs of the wrought iron balconies, the way corners turned up on the roofs of some of the palaces, the city squares. It all whispered of Havana and Cartagena de Indias, of China and Brazil—places that in turn had adopted Portuguese touches.

The sixteenth-century historian Gaspar Frutuosa dubbed the Azores the "universal port of call," and Angra was the main harbor.

There are two steady winds that circle the earth. The air blows counterclockwise in the Northern Hemisphere and clockwise in the Southern Hemisphere: the trade winds. In the seafaring era, routes depended on those winds and the ocean currents. The only way to take a galleon filled with gold and silver from the New World back to Europe passed through the Azores. Angra has always been a crossroads, and there's a special magic to places where they mix things up.

The lights from boats in the marina made squiggly colored lines on the water. Moonlight gleamed on the black-and-white patterns of the cobblestone street in front of the hotel. There was a devastating earthquake in the 1980s, and I'm told they tried to put every cobblestone in the city back in its original place.

I was too jet-lagged to sleep, and I wanted to be out there. I asked Grace, the clerk at the desk, whether there was anywhere safe for me to walk at two in the morning.

She looked confused. "You can walk anywhere you want to walk," she said. "Don't worry. It's safe—it's still early by the Portuguese way of thinking!"

Terceira has crime in the form of domestic violence, drug smuggling, and even theft, but random violence is pretty much unknown.

I strolled over to the main square and ate a pistachio gelato while listening to a man play an Eric Clapton song on the guitar. Then I felt pulled to a long stretch of seawall. The ocean side was piled with the same giant concrete in the shape of jacks used all over the world to break up the force of waves. A lot of times they are stamped with numbers, as if there were some giant child determined to keep track of his toys, but it's so engineers can monitor the jacks' placement from aerial photographs. I strolled to the end of the wall, almost dreamy, climbed out on the boulders on the harbor side, and sat in darkness looking back at the gently glowing city. I felt unconcerned when footsteps passed by on the walk above.

At home I didn't make much of the fact that I was always a bit on guard: walking to my car, keys out in case I needed to gouge a bad guy. It was just part of the way things were. I once interviewed a young man who came from Stockton, California, and went to Stanford, near the elegant confines of rich Palo Alto. He said the most startling thing he learned at the prestigious school was that hearing gunfire all night wasn't normal for other people.

Just being here, at ease, alone in the dark, made me realize I had been mindlessly maneuvering just-the-way-things-are, accepting that violence was always a possibility, never realizing there are other places where it doesn't feel that way. Of course, my dad had a saying for this: "They might have a different way of doing things across the river." Or in this case, the middle of the ocean.

I liked the idea of my own, personal Tenth Island, made only of things I wanted to keep. I'd start by carrying inside me a place where a desk clerk looked confused when a woman asked where it was safe for her to walk alone.

On the way back, I passed two men. Don't worry. This is not taking some dire turn where I turn off the inner safety detector and am immediately the missing victim whose driver's license is shown on the evening news.

One of the men, the tall one, said, *"Boa noite."*

"Boa noite," I replied, this falling within my twenty words of the native vocabulary.

He immediately rattled off several sentences I didn't understand.

"*Não falo português*"—"I don't speak Portuguese," I said.

"Well, then," he said, switching to English, "we'll have to teach you."

He introduced himself as a fire chief. But I misunderstood and thought his first name was Chef, which would become my nickname for him. When he was younger, before he was married and a man of responsibility, he learned English from American TV shows to woo the Portuguese American girls who came over every summer. He was tall now, but he'd been scrawny and short then. He figured it was his only way to compete.

He said the most terrifying moment of his life came at thirteen, when one of the objects of his flirtations showed up where he and his friends were camping. She crawled into his sleeping bag. He wasn't ready for such a victory. He wiggled out of the bag and ran the whole way to his house, jumping a couple of low rock walls on the way, feeling as though he was in flight. He still remembers the smell of mint that his feet unleashed running across the fields and soaring through the air, exhilarated by his close brush with the unknown.

The mainland relative he was showing around had drunk too much *aguardente—água* ("water") + *ardente* ("fiery") = fire water—or in American terms, moonshine. He was lying on a bench.

"Help me babysit," Chef said. "I love my island and I know everyone. I can tell you anything you want to know." He'd already known there was an American writer on Terceira because, he said, it was a very little island.

He browsed the contacts on his phone. "Oh, this guy is starting an ecology museum—you have to talk to him," he said, beginning to dial.

"It's three a.m.," I said.

"Hmm, I suppose he could be asleep," Chef said, looking doubtful.

As a lifelong night owl, I appreciated that it was in question.

The relative sat up. He held a finger in the air as if testing wind direction. He cleared his throat. "The wonderful thing about the Azores is that they have people who love the sea more than big houses and nice cars," he announced.

I asked him why he lived in Lisbon if he liked Terceira so much.

"Because I have a big house and a nice car," he said, and lay back down.

Ta-choo, Ta-choo

The hotel where I was staying was small and elegant. Gleaming wood banisters, stone stairs, and waiters who wore tuxedos. The restaurant had a balcony overlooking the bay where a buffet was served in the mornings. As a nod to American and Canadian eating habits, there were scrambled eggs, sausages, and pancakes in chafing pans in the corner.

But I liked the Portuguese breakfast at my free digs. There was always fresh cheese made on the island. It was soft and mild but with just a hint of tang so that you had to take another bite to try to pin down the flavor. It was made from the milk of the cows that were everywhere, walking down the middle of roads, posing by hedges of blue hydrangeas. The only traffic jams I had seen in Terceira were because of cows crossing the street at milking time. An array of breads awaited the cheese: thick crust, chewy inside; thick crust, fluffy inside; and sweet breads of varying sweetness. There were meats, yogurts, pastries, cereals, and an assortment of tropical fruits. But as far as I was concerned, bread, cheese, a few local grapes, and one of the little Portuguese espressos called *cafés* were the point of the production.

The same three waiters, all older gentlemen, worked all three meals. I was there only in the mornings for the food included in the hotel bill, but the waiters would wave to me when I left the hotel while they were setting the tables for lunch. Later, if I happened to pass by again while strolling about the historic city, they would wave even if they were in the middle of taking an order. In the evenings before the dinner rush, they would be on the balcony watching the sea, and I'd be heading out to the seawall, and we would shout greetings. They were cleaning up when I came back at night, and we'd always exchange a *"Boa noite."*

We had introduced ourselves, but the unfamiliar sounds left me knowing only that all the waiters' names had the sound *zhhh* somewhere in the syllables. I relied on custom, simply calling each of them *señor.* It felt as if it had a nicer connotation than saying "Hey, man" or even "Sir" in the United States.

Tourism at this time was still a trickle of people, and as a non-Portuguese American with no ties to the military base on the other side of the island, I was a novelty. Lucky for me because the waiters' attention made me feel known. I liked having people to greet when I came "home."

Chef, the fire chief who knew everyone, was taking Terceira ambassador duties seriously. He lived in some village on the other side of the island, but most days he would roar to Angra, in the red Mustang he had been driving since he was seventeen, to fetch and deliver me to someone he thought I should meet if I wanted to understand the Azores. We visited a goatherd, a fisherman, a museum curator, and a man who was 101 years old but spoke lucidly and poetically if Chef's translations were to be believed.

Chef did not think my planned two-week stay was long enough to understand Terceira. He told me he had an unfinished garage out in his garden that he could turn into an apartment, and I could move in, and he was sure his wife and children wouldn't mind at all if I ate meals at their house. He strongly felt it was time for the outside world to know more about the Azores. It was a generous offer but did not match my goals. I wasn't exactly sure what my goals were, but American-living-in-garage-who-comes-to-the-main-house-for-free-meals was not an immediate contender.

José and Luisa were also enthusiastic guides. They had a speedboat, and in the afternoons, as soon as José came back from his job as a television repairman and Luisa returned from her office job, we headed out on the ocean. Usually we went to what they called Parrot Cove. José would cut the engines, and the boat became our diving board. We'd jump, feeling that whooshing moment that turns everyone into a seven-year-old. We would surface from the cold, salty water gasping and laughing and swim beneath the cliffs of a small islet. I always scanned the birds flying overhead for some of the namesake parrots. It was only when I looked at a map later that I understood they were saying *pirate*.

I didn't speak Portuguese. José spoke little English I could understand. But he grew so agitated at not being understood that I just nodded yes at whatever he said. Luisa's English came in two sentence structures: "I like . . . [noun or verb]" or "I do not like . . . [noun or verb]," a strategy I would adopt when I finally picked up a little Portuguese.

But it was amazing how much information was shared with mugging, drawing, saying single words, and getting help from random bilingual bystanders. Even with little common language, I learned that José and Luisa were in a second marriage for both. They were in love. They were happy. José attributed this to two things:

- Luisa was very beautiful.
- They meditated every night.

José had bought books on the internet about brain waves (or at least that's what I understood through pantomime) and learned how to meditate from videotapes.

One night I left the hotel at what would have been considered late in some world I used to live in, which didn't suit my timetable. I was headed to the seawall to watch the ocean. It may have been my form of meditation. I passed couple after couple. A Noah's Ark of twosomes paraded around the plaza. I felt a twinge of hurt at being left out.

At the end of the jetty, a man was sitting on the rock that was my usual spot. I started to turn around, but he said, "Don't go. Look how many chairs are in my living room."

I perched on another rock, and we began the pitter-patter of verbal jousting. But to me the situation was funnier than the banter. Because, you see, things like this don't happen. You don't walk out the door, start feeling definitively alone, and then find yourself sitting on a rock, joking around with a handsome Portuguese man while looking at city lights on the water. Unless, of course, you are on an island.

We walked back to the harbor. We were standing in front of my hotel. The banter was becoming halting, turning into weighted pauses. A slow magnet pull set in, and our faces started creeping closer. I thought, *He's going to kiss me*, in a heart-beating he's-going-to-kiss-me way I had not felt since adolescence.

Midjourney, with our faces still about a foot apart, he grabbed my hand and put it on his chest, and said, "Can you feel how fast my heart is beating? It is not this way since I was a teenager."

"No! Me too," I said.

We started talking about how wasn't it strange that you could lose such a feeling and never even realize it was gone. And now to have it with a stranger. Was it because we were strangers, or was there something inexplicable at work? Did things that can't be explained exist?

It was intellectually stimulating, but I wondered what had become of the kiss.

Then he said, "Listen to the sound of the waves."

We listened to the water slowly hitting the seawall: *ta-choo, ta-choo, ta-choo.*

He said nothing more.

So we listened some more. *Ta-choo, ta-choo, ta-choo . . . ta-choo, ta-choo.*

He *still* said nothing.

We were both standing sideways, cocking our ears to the sea.

Then he said, "It is the perfect rhythm for making love."

Oh.

But there was more.

"Concentrate on your elbow."

Excuse me? I thought. *Was that Portuguese and it sounded like "Concentrate on your elbow" in English?*

But no, he had been reading a book about the power of the mind. It said you could amplify feelings. He told me that I must put all my feelings into my elbow, to concentrate very hard on my elbow.

OK, whatever. I concentrated very hard on my elbow. There were tingles. Although I wouldn't put elbows high on my list of tingly parts.

"You can use the same technique with other parts," he said.

We were starting to move in for another kiss, but my mind was now wondering whether this was OK, whether it was *really* over with whichever on-and-off relationship I was involved in at the time. (Since I long ago swore off anything on-and-off, earlier follies have become an indistinguishable blur of romantic ambiguities.) It was then, as we were just about to kiss, that I noticed all three waiters and the busboy standing on the balcony watching the scene unfold.

"The waiters!" I said.

It dawned on me that a lot of people on the island knew who I was, and they gossiped regularly with their counterparts in California. Maybe I ought to act like a respectable journalist and not some lonely heart on vacation.

"The waiters," I said again. "I have to go inside." And I left.

Years later, I met this same man in mainland Portugal. He told me that he had thought "The waiters!" was an American colloquialism he wasn't familiar with and spent the next summer asking visiting relatives what it meant.

What I find most surprising looking back at my first introduction to Terceira is that I remember all the highlight moments—the almost kiss, swimming in Pirate Cove, dancing with Alberto—as if I am watching a film. It unfolds before me, and I am a spectator. But the moments I recall in a way that grabs me by my heels and transports me through time and space until I am there, able to smell the sea and feel the breeze, are ones that I regretted at that time as wasted.

My first week on the island, I didn't get up and out the door until after noon. I would wake up and listen to people climbing the stairs to breakfast and smell coffee and hear childish squeals as the small beach in front of the hotel began to fill. For hours I would try to chide myself into motion: "You have crossed an ocean, you are in a city designated by the United Nations as a site of world cultural significance, there are people out there, possibilities—get up!"

But I propped up in bed on white pillows watching the flutter of the curtain on the French door to my room's small balcony, half thinking thoughts I still half remember. I have a theory (of course).

The Importance of Dawdling Theory

> This theory holds that there is nothing more valuable than time to waste. The most interesting things are the ones tucked in the empty spaces to be discovered when dawdling, loitering, lying in bed. It's the only part of the universe you can truly call your own.

Such a theory coming from the likes of me—admittedly lazy and never a morning person—could rightfully be considered self-serving and suspect. But in the 1930s, Lin Yutang, a Chinese writer, translator, and linguist, published *The Importance of Living*, one of the most influential books of its time. I came upon this book through another book called *Books for Living* by Will Schwalbe, who wrote odes to the books he'd found most useful. He highlighted this excerpt:

I believe one of the greatest pleasures of life is to curl up one's legs in bed. The posture of the arms is also very important in order to reach the greatest degree of aesthetic pleasure and mental power. I believe the best posture is not lying flat on the bed, but being upholstered with big soft pillows at an angle of thirty degrees with either one arm or both arms placed behind the back of one's head. In this posture any poet can write immortal poetry, any philosopher can revolutionize human thought, and any scientist can make epoch-making discoveries.

I had not yet read this when I was whiling away a good chunk of my first visit to the Azores. Yet somehow in that little seaside hotel, I followed Lin Yutang's precise instructions for "the greatest degree of aesthetic pleasure and mental power."

Bull on a Rope

Filomena and Gladys, my Cuban Portuguese instructor from the flight over, left an invitation at the hotel for me to go to a *tourada à corda* with them. I accepted, since I was in Terceira and this form of bullfighting is a hundred percent Terceiran tradition—but I had a sense of trepidation.

We drove through several seaside villages of white houses with trims the color of Christmas ribbons until we got to the village that had this night's turn at hosting a bullfight. The streets were hung with white lights, and the crowd was packed so tightly, we could hardly weave our way through the commotion. Homeowners were already nailing up the entrances to their property. The custom is that if you are not an invited guest, you find a house and ask whether you can come into the yard to watch the fight. The owners of the first house Filomena asked (since she was the one who spoke Portuguese understood by others) said yes. I was squeezed between a group of teenage Portuguese girls singing American pop songs and a group who may have been their grandmothers all sitting on a wall. The wall was about four feet tall, not as high as I would have liked. Bulls can clear eight feet easily. I knew that from living in an agricultural part of California where the occasional "bull on the loose with police in pursuit" scenario would play on the newsroom scanner.

There was the warning boom, and people scurried this way and that to get into houses and walled yards. A few minutes later, another boom, and the bull was in the street, judging by the men running in the other direction from the bull crate.

The bull appeared on the section of road in front of us. Every time the bull so much as swiveled its head in our direction, I jumped off the wall. It was instinctive: Bull glance. Diana down. One of the older women scowled at me. With each preemptive hop, I was jumping into her garden, although I was trying to be mindful of the plants. I decided that I would stand my ground like the other women by staying seated come what may, even if that was a bull closer to me than I preferred.

The bull swerved, running in our direction and back toward the *pastores*—the men holding the ropes tied to the bull, a futile endeavor in this configuration. One of the *pastores* jumped up on the wall, and I leaned over to make room for him. A beautiful teenage girl on the other side pushed him back into the street. "You move for no one but the bull," she told me with a toss of her glossy hair.

Once the bull passed, I couldn't see the action down the street. There was screaming coming from somewhere out of sight. Heads craned as people watched for the bull to return. By the time it did, its sides heaved with heavy panting. Thick, foamy spittle hung from its mouth. Men flapped towels and yelled. Some in the crowd who had been hanging back were now bolder, stomping their feet at the exhausted animal. Only when the *pastores* surrounded the bull to herd it back into the crate did it roar, its eyes flashing in what looked to me like angry terror.

This whole episode was repeated three times, with three different bulls. There was a lot of waiting—waiting for the bull to be put into the crate, waiting for the traffic piled up on the one main road on the island to be allowed through during the break between animals. I suspected the lengthy pauses were far from dull to the teenage girls near me. They elbowed one another and giggled as various young men passed, along with the soda and candy bar vendors.

I knew the fourth and final bull was bigger, faster, and more aggressive before I even saw it. A man behind me yelled to some nearby children, "Get away from the fence. Now!" He said it in Portuguese, but I knew exactly what he was saying. I checked with Filomena, and I'd got it verbatim.

Two men in the street worked in tandem, holding their umbrellas together in front of the bull. When the bull charged, they each twirled apart, and the bull ran between them. The crowd went crazy, clapping and pounding walls. It must have caught the bull's attention. He turned and charged the wall across from us, and about fifty people tumbled backward in a heap, their legs flying in the air. I felt guilty about laughing, but Frank's book was right: the bullfight did create situations both comical and dramatic. No one seemed hurt, and I wondered whether this was because people had been drinking through three bulls already and most of them were as floppy as rabbit ears.

Touradas à corda usually have three or four bulls. They say the fifth bull is the hangover the next day. I was alarmed by how drunk some of the men in the street were, although I supposed they would sober up fast if they found themselves in the bull's sights.

I was wrong.

The bull singled out a sweaty fat man. Judging from his surf-style clothes, I took him to be a Portuguese immigrant from California. The man ran to our wall, one of the lower ones, and leaped. But unlike the agile *pastores*, he didn't make it. He hung on the wall, his head and shoulders flapping down next to me, his ample bum sticking out into the street, a real bull's-eye. A few of us grabbed his arms and tried to pull him over the wall, but he thought the whole thing was hysterical—he was a bag of giggling, drunken deadweight. The bull was moving its head back and forth. I felt a little sick. I was about to see someone gored.

The man was half on and half off the wall. The bull lowered its head—and the two guys from earlier jumped in front of the bull. They waved red umbrellas on both sides of it. Still the bull focused on Mr. Pincushion, who was chortling and reeked of beer and sweat. Finally the movement of one of the umbrellas caught the bull's attention. It turned its head. He charged the umbrella. The man holding the umbrella ran in a circle, then easily leaped over the wall on the other side of the street—a jump the bull could not make without a straight charge. The animal loped down the street. As soon as the bull was out of sight, the women and I looked at the man we had been trying to save in clear disgust, as if we wished he had been gored. I can still picture his maniacally laughing face.

Videos of the bullfights were an industry. Walking the cobblestone streets of Angra the next day, I noted all the highlight reels playing in shop windows and bars. Endless loops of men being thrown and gored and searching for their eyeglasses after a stomping.

I met Chef for tea at the plaza overlooking the beach where a few weeks earlier there had been a big bullfight. I'd seen the footage of a rampaging bull swimming out and tipping over a rowboat full of teenagers. Chef wanted to know what I thought of my first bullfight.

I told him I felt sorry for the bull.

Diving Board Notes

A couple of days later, I was back in California, back through Alice's looking glass, Narnia's wardrobe entrance, Harry Potter's Platform 9¾, and any other portals where the protagonist is deposited back to his or her old reality. I wondered whether all that fantastical stuff had really happened.

Clearly, I needed to return to the Azores.

I had a plan. Before accepting Frank's offer, before I ever went to Terceira, I had first tried to get a journalism grant to write about the Azorean diaspora. The form rejection letter I'd received included a handwritten note at the bottom telling me that there had been support for the project and that I was encouraged to apply the following year. A handwritten "we're sorry, but" note before I had even visited the islands? I counted it as a triumph. Surely I would get it this time.

I spent weekends exploring Azorean California towns, driving to Tulare and Turlock and Hilmar. I sent off my second application and waited.

The Manly Author was trying to understand my obsession. His theory was that maybe I was secretly Portuguese despite looking nothing like it. My heritage was a mystery. I had no definite ethnicity, and to the Manly Author, everything was a matter of blood. He was Armenian, and he attributed his intense nature to his people being from the ancient Armenian village of Moosh, now in eastern Turkey.

I reported this back to the family of Armenians who had long ago enfolded me in their Fresno clan. I thought it was ridiculous.

"Oh no. This is right," said patriarch Armen. "He is an angry man?"

"Well, I think it's more like righteous indignation, trying to set the world straight," I said.

"No," said Armen. "People from Moosh are just plain mad."

I didn't think DNA defined me, but I did start thinking that Manly Author might be onto something. Maybe it *was* about family. The Hamayelians were my tribe even if they did call me their *odar*—"other."

I first met them when Odie and Armen had a mom-and-pop diner in downtown Fresno. I often sat at their counter happily eating my kabob while Armen badgered me. He would tell me I looked stressed and that I should have a man supporting me so I could stay home. He just liked to see me get flabbergasted, which I knew, but I always did anyway. One day it came up that I had no family, husband or otherwise, in California. Odie, the matriarch, almost dropped a cup. They searched out eye contact with each other as if I'd told them I was from another planet. It was inconceivable to them that a person could live her life alone. Soon they were inviting me to breakfast and tea and Thanksgiving dinner.

Now, I had been taking the stuffing to Thanksgivings for a decade, although I vastly preferred their Persian rice with orange peel. Their little diner was gone, in its place a parking lot for a federal courthouse. But theirs was the house where I drank countless cups of tea and floated in a backyard pool while we chewed over the day's happenings.

Armen and Odie ended up in America with their three sons, Patrick, Reni, and Arby, because they were on vacation in Pennsylvania in 1979 when Iran took Americans hostage, and suddenly their passports were worthless.

Armenians settled in Iran (then Persia) hundreds of years before the genocide that killed 1.5 million Armenians in the Ottoman Empire between 1915 and 1917. In Iran before the revolution, Armenians were allowed their own religion and schools, accepted by their Muslim neighbors, and left to live in peace for at least four hundred years. This is why, according to Armen, Armenian Persians were of a less morose temperament than the Armenians in Fresno, whose generations traced to Armenia and the genocide.

Armen, a man of gentle humor when not trying to provoke me with absurd sexist tropes, told me how traditional and stern he had been in Iran. He said that Odie had to ask his permission to even visit her mother. It was the way things were. "But then I got here, and I saw men be nice and soft to their families, and I thought, *Ah, this is a better way*," he recalled.

They had lived in Fresno for more than thirty years, but Odie still had dreams in which she could smell the fresh soft lavash delivered each morning and see the snow on Mount Alborz and the sun on the Caspian Sea. Armen liked to show me photos of a modern, vibrant Tehran before the last Islamic revolution.

In the Central Valley, each distant war and famine and dictatorship brought a new wave of immigrants to factory fields. Nothing is as global as a California farm town.

I wrote about people who missed going to Mass in a stone church in Mexican mountains, walking through rice paddies in Laos, and reading poetry in their elaborate garden in Afghanistan. They yearned for lemongrass, banana trees, "real" chilies, adobe houses, carved temples, tiled mosques, the Rio Grande, nopales, rose water, pillowy samosas, and moonshine that tasted of flowers before leaving you dead-drunk. I was surrounded by the displaced. Most of what these people missed was lost forever to them, unlike the Azores, where the diaspora could pop in for summer visits.

My fascination with being able to return might even have had something to do with my own life. The night my father died of lung cancer—when I was sixteen, when my family had already moved to cheaper and cheaper places in the face of medical bills we couldn't pay, until we lived in a rented house with bars on the windows in a neighborhood pocketed between highway on-ramps—I ran. I had never been much of a runner. I was slow and given to shin splints. Nevertheless, I ran. I ran past the liquor store and the apartment complexes with names conjuring the orange groves they replaced: Citrus Flats, Orange Blossom Manor, the Groves. They all had banners promoting "First Month's Rent Free!" just in case you couldn't tell by looking that no one with a choice would want to live there.

I ran until my heart pounded in my ears and my legs trembled and my lungs burned. I ran until I got to one of those small parks that cities make developers put in to offset building ugly apartment complexes where there used to be orange groves. I threw myself down on the grass. And I felt my breath and my thumping heart with my whole body.

I could feel the ground supporting me, and above me the stars stretched into the endless void that had taken my father. It was a vast feeling. *I'm alive*, I thought, marveling at my own breath, now stamped forever with the knowledge of how tenuous it was. How tenuous it is. I closed my eyes and felt myself a speck but part of a universe you can sense revolving if you just stop.

A year later, my mother, Beverly, died of Lou Gehrig's disease, but even the doctors blamed a broken heart on her rapid decline. Though I again felt a connection to something huge and beyond me, I was also set loose from everything familiar. And ever since, I've worried that in this great swirl of connecting dots, there isn't a dot where I belong. I feared I was doomed to free float. It was the reason I liked immigration stories: place and separation and identity and figuring out what stayed put even when you didn't.

I tuned back into the conversation with Armen. He was still going through Armenian villages and the personality traits their descendants magically possessed three thousand years later. There was the village of the bossy, the village of the caustic, and even a village of heavy calves, although I don't think that can be defined as a personality trait.

No wonder I felt right at home earlier that week when a young Californian who had never been to the Azores explained to me that he partied because his grandparents came from Terceira. "You know the saying: 'There are eight islands and the party that is Terceira!' It's in my blood," he said. On his arm he had a tattoo of the island where he had never been.

Aileen—Patrick's wife, Odie and Armen's daughter-in-law—was usually my ally against destiny by tribe, but she chimed in with Armen. It didn't matter, she said, that her nickname was Mouse because her father's village was Kazaz, so she was a very courageous mouse. People from Kazaz are known to be brave.

One of the first times Aileen and I met, she told me that the most fun time of her life had been when she was an Armenian Iranian refugee in Spain. She wasn't allowed to work or go to school, so she took flamenco dance. That day she taught me some steps. I taught her jazz hands (not an even trade), and I knew that I really wanted to hold on to a friend who could make refugee status a lark.

The funny thing was that, for all their talk of Armenians being this way, Persians being that—don't get them started on plain old Americans—Odie and Armen's stories were almost always testaments to individuals not being easily stereotyped.

Odie was pregnant with Arby in Tehran during the Islamic Revolution. She went to bed early to try to sleep through the worst of the demonstrations. But every night, the neighbors went to their roof, shot guns in the air, and shouted, "Death to America!"

She went over to their house. "Doesn't your religion say, 'If you make your neighbor unhappy, you make God unhappy'?" she asked her Muslim neighbors. "Well, I'm unhappy. Every night you scare me."

They apologized, and after that they always came over, knocked on the door, and politely warned her when they were going to the roof to shoot guns and yell, "Death to Americans," so she wouldn't be startled. They had to do it, they explained. The other neighbors might report them as not being loyal revolutionaries if they didn't, and they were trying to keep a low profile while they tried to immigrate to the United States.

It was surprising that I knew the stories so well because one thing I had learned from hanging out with the Hamayelian clan is that in an extended family it sometimes seems as if no one listens.

The Christmas before, I snuck away from dinner, went out on the diving board, and wrote down what passed for conversation while I still had hold of every word.

Diving Board Notes

> Odie tells Albert, a friend the family knew back in Iran, that I had a cocktail party, and they met my Armenian writer friend, and she found him intelligent and smokin' hot. Odie is perfectly fluent in English, but connotation can still trip her up. A while back, I told her that when Americans think someone is nice-looking, they say, "smokin' hot."
>
> Albert's twenty-two-year-old son seated next to me whispers, "She thinks he's smoking hot?"
>
> I whisper back, "She also thinks you and I are smoking hot. It's her phrase."

Albert, on the other side of me, whispers, "You are smoking pot?"

Patrick, across from me, listening through the din, says, "No, I don't like smoking pot."

Armen, a little hard of hearing, says to Patrick, "You like smoking pot?!"

Albert whispers to me, "Pot is not so bad. I like Scotch better."

Odie, oblivious to their side conversations, finishes her recounting with a flourish: "And he's such a good writer!"

Knowing I'd sat through many such conversations, you might think their house would be the last place I would go when the letter arrived telling me whether I got the grant. But I drove straight there, the letter unopened. During dinner I opened it under the table and looked. I didn't get the money. My heart sank—it's not just a cliché; something in the general vicinity of my chest dropped to my stomach. In my mind's eye I was watching myself go to the newspaper office the next day and the next, never leaving the office to report and tell stories but sitting at a desk beneath fluorescent lights, churning out blog posts at an ever-quickening pace. I willed someone at the table to ask me whether I had heard about the grant but otherwise sat mute. I couldn't cough up the words. Finally, Odie asked me whether I'd heard anything.

"I didn't get it," I almost whispered.

"Well, then, you didn't want it," said Odie. "And I don't like them."

"What's this?" said Armen.

"Some organization that isn't good didn't choose her island thing," Odie said.

"Island?" said Patrick. "What islands are those? Azores? Do they have coral reefs?"

"Coral reefs are too, too interesting," said Armen. "They are very important."

"You know what?" Patrick told me. "You should try again, but this time find islands with coral reefs."

"Don't go to the same people," said Odie. "I don't like them. But reefs are interesting. Lots of things live in them."

Aileen didn't say anything. She just met my disappointment with mute sympathy as, all around us, it was decided I should study coral reefs.

So, Fly

You adapt. You joke with your friends. You hike on the weekends, and you don't spend all your time thinking about how you stumbled onto something you could really throw yourself into, but instead you are sitting in an office on a chair that swivels and adjusts up and down in a vain attempt to soothe your body's screaming from forced inactivity, and you are writing trend stories that you are embarrassed to see your name on.

You might even nose around the many issues of coral reefs.

It wasn't that I had forgotten the Azores and their connection with California that was part of a whole kitten-string ball of US immigration, but I was always on deadline and most concerned with whatever was due next.

One day I was slouched at my desk typing. I had moved over to the features department and was doling out tips on making New Year's resolutions. I was wondering how I was going to make a story interesting to read when it was so boring to write that I started doing lazy 360s in my swivel chair. There was the ding of an email notification, and I opened a note from Chef. "Happy New Ear!" it read, since it was January and he wasn't as proficient with his written English as his spoken. I could smell the ocean. I could hear Chef's laugh. I wrote him back and told him I hoped he had been diving in the sea that day and that he never, ever sat beneath fluorescent lights.

Barbara, my best work chum, was worried about me. My nickname for Barbara was Taz because she could work herself up into delivering hysterically funny rants about the world with the energy of a Tasmanian devil. Lately she had set the world aside to sermonize about my not making proper use of my talents. She thought I needed to find writing I cared about—a calling. This was easier said than done. Since kindergarten I had been a generalist. Even then I envied those who lived for butterflies or spent every recess perfecting their kickball skills. That's one of the reasons journalism *was* my calling. I found everything pretty interesting but had no particular callings.

It was finally prayer that got me out of my doldrums and back to the Azores. Not mine. Ron's.

Ron was the newspaper's religion writer. He was an exceedingly kind man who favored a healthy spray of cologne, wore a massive jeweled ring commemorating the Fresno State Women's Softball National Championship of 1998, and led Bible study in the conference room when it wasn't being used for blood sport budget meetings during which they decided what belonged on the front page. I thought of Ron as his own church, complete with incense, bling, and a call to pray. Ron loved his job. He got to go to a different church, a different faith, every Sunday and write about it.

I was surprised to hear he was going to apply for a buyout. He was looking at missionary work. Our paper had a union, and according to the rules, all could apply, but first dibs went to those with the most years on the job. Ron was a sure thing. I was down on the list in the not-a-chance category, but I filled out the application just to remind myself I should be working harder on leaving and finding a place where I belonged.

All across the country, newspapers were downsizing and reporting jobs were disappearing. At first, at the *Fresno Bee*, we watched from a detached distance. We were the only newspaper in our region. It was part of a chain that prided itself on being family controlled and community based and having weathered many hard times without ever laying off a single reporter or photographer.

In the meantime, outside the Central Valley, investors forced Knight Ridder, one of the nation's biggest newspaper chains, with a string of Pulitzers, to make waves of newsroom cuts. By 2006, Wall Street was demanding it be sold. McClatchy, the *Fresno Bee*'s parent company, bought Knight Ridder for $4.5 billion in cash and stock and the assumption of $2 billion in debt. It was a case of a smaller fish swallowing a whale. McClatchy immediately put any Knight Ridder newsroom with a union up for sale. And now even in Fresno, we were on our third round of downsizing.

I trudged into the office the morning the buyouts would be completed—or layoffs, if too many people changed their minds and backed out. I knew that even if I stayed, the times I got to wander and explore would be gone. No more little slice-of-life stories. The goal now was stories that would zing around the web. The one time I attained "going viral" status was when I wrote an uplifting tale about two boys in a rough part of the city starting a shaved-ice stand. I thought it was the common humanity in the story sending those numbers spiking, but our young, internet-savvy receptionist, Heather, pointed out it was all the people searching "shaved" because Britney Spears had flashed her shorn privates that day.

I stopped by Barbara's desk and told her that I foresaw unending days of pounding out things like "Man Stabbed in Porterville," inadvertently making Porterville sound like a body part. My desk was next to Ron's. There was a crowd around him. He was telling colleagues that he wasn't taking the buyout. He'd been up all night praying and he felt God still had meaningful work for him at the paper. I checked my email. Barbara had messaged, "They're going by department, not paper, for seniority!" Ron and I were in the same small remnants of a features department.

There was another message from an editor asking me to come to his office. He offered me the buyout, and I signed the papers. I had no plan. I hadn't really thought it was a possibility. My dad's saying for such a time . . . there wasn't one. My father did not believe in quitting one job before you had another. But my mom went around the house singing that happy song about "even though we ain't got money," so . . . maybe there was, somewhere in the universe, support for a leap that made no financial sense.

I grabbed my keys and drove to Armen and Odie's. Armen was at the computer playing a card game. I told him I'd taken a buyout for twenty weeks of pay.

"This is not very long," he said.

"Oh God. I made a mistake, didn't I?" I asked, starting to breathe a little faster.

"This you cannot know until the future," he said, "and maybe not for sure even then." Armen had often worried about my being an unmarried woman. He now pointed to it as a saving grace. "You have no husband that you must tell of this news and no children to feed." So there was that: no children would go hungry, only me.

It was only me on all fronts. I didn't even qualify for a credit card after an earlier stint as an unsuccessful freelance writer. I'd been trying to save departure money, since the Alpaugh fight had left all my trust at work broken, but every time I got a little pile, it got chopped back down for new tires or taxes or other things I probably should have planned on.

Odie was in the kitchen making my favorite Persian Armenian salad: butter leaf lettuce, boiled potato, jicama, olive oil, and lemon. As she tossed the greens, I poured out a whole dramatic monologue about it being not just about my job but also my grief over what was happening to journalism. What would we all be without our stories and without a source of common knowledge? I was really waxing up to full oration. I may have declared that democracy dies in darkness before the *Washington Post* did.

Odie, who had lost an entire country and previous life, rolled her eyes. "Oh, Princess. They cut the tree down. You have wings, so fly." (Odie and Armen always gave people nicknames. When they first met me, they wanted to call me Bambi because they found me gawky and brown eyed like a deer. I protested that Bambi sounded like a moniker used by prostitutes. They then went with Princess because of my supposedly exceedingly good posture. I figured I didn't get two vetoes, and that is why I have the nickname of a French poodle.)

Maybe I already had the thought before Odie's advice. But I like the idea that I took her literally. The day after I picked up my we'll-pay-you-to-leave check, I bought a ticket to fly back to the Azores.

I wish I could figure out the rules that the universe follows for catching you when you jump off a cliff. There seems to be some sort of caveat that the life rafts won't line up until after you're hurtling through the air spread out for a belly flop.

Before I did it myself, I could not figure out a way to finance a long trip to Terceira, just because I felt there was *something* about it—something to be understood. Now I looked at Craigslist for ideas on how to word an advertisement looking for someone to live in Fresno in the summer, when it gets to be 104 degrees. There was a Santa Barbara river researcher looking for a place the very summer I would be gone. Matt sublet my house (don't tell my landlord). He would stay at least until September.

I called Elmano, the head of a Portuguese Studies Program in California. He had been the academic source on the application for the grant I didn't get. I asked him whether he knew anyone who might be renting out a place in Terceira. He told me I could stay in his family home for free—they often lent it to friends. I had never met him in person. I told him I had no firm plan. I didn't know exactly what

I wanted to write about and had no organization behind me. He said the offer still stood.

It is only in retrospect, now that Elmano and his wife, Albertina, are longtime friends, that I realize how striking this conversation was. The words *no firm plan* are a foreign concept to Elmano and Albertina. She has taught kindergarten for more than twenty years. She will ask a car full of adults whether they have used the restroom before the trip. She will pass out umbrellas if there is more than a 20 percent chance of rain. Once, at a party at their house, my date for the evening noticed a long to-do list on the kitchen wall.

"Wow, all of that in one month?" he asked.

It was for one week.

A longtime friend of theirs chimed in. "Oh, that's nothing. I came over here once when the two boys were small, and they had 'have sex' on the list," he said.

Albertina shrugged. "Hey, if it's not on the list, it doesn't get done," she said.

This level of organization unnerves me. But I am a stalwart fan of lists.

Azores writing ideas:

- California culture
    - Subcultures?
    - Dairy stuff?
- Bump into something.

Kiss and Tell

There is an expectation that books involving travel that are written by a woman will be more personal than those written by a man, with a great deal of dishing about one's love life (or lack thereof). I think it's unfair that one gender is expected to kiss and tell while the other gender is allowed to kiss and keep it quiet. But that being said, I may as well get some use out of what at the time was a pathetic track record.

I had dated a pilot afraid of buttons. He'd been trapped in a duvet as a child. One friend of mine didn't think this was a deal breaker, likening it to her mother's aversion to plaid: "It makes her dizzy. She has to leave the room." Then it came out that he didn't like zippers either, and I realized he just wanted people to keep their clothes on.

There had been an anthropologist who was almost driven to tears when my friend Shellee and I joked that we must be descended from Mediterranean climes, since we liked to lounge in hammocks. "It's like you haven't even *read* Margaret Mead," he spluttered. "You are propagating imperial theory! You are undermining individual agency!" (Or something along those lines.) He broke up with me the night before I was to throw him a birthday luncheon. He told me my light shone too bright for him.

I cried on the shoulder of my friend Jeanne, who grew up in a black church, and she whipped out her best gospel choir–style oration. "That's right, and you just *shine, shine, shine*, girl. And remember that little man isn't even a bed light."

I invited Jack Moody, my coworker down the street, to drop in and help me eat the leftovers from the party for thirty that had been canceled. Moody loved to eat. He came by at lunch every day for a week and, over cedar-plank salmon, pilaf, and grilled vegetables, said, "I am *so* glad that short professor dumped you."

I had fallen into a dark, unrelenting thrall with a fly fisherman whom I thought had the sexiest slow voice I had ever heard and whom all my girlfriends thought sounded perennially drugged. I just couldn't keep away from him. Even though it was clear he was best kept away from. Moody knew the guy and pestered me by impersonating his laconic, late-night radio voice. "Helloooo, I'm Ricco Suave-ay," he'd say, in an accurate vocal rendition.

Moody had no room to talk. Barbara, who had known him since they had both worked together at another paper, called his postdivorce string of romances "disposable women." "He won't date anyone who might be as smart as him," she told me.

I relayed that to Moody, and he wasn't offended; he agreed. "I'm committed to bachelorhood," he said. "Talk to me after you've been married and divorced."

I was finally able to break Suave's spell by listening to Johnny Cash's "Ring of Fire" fourteen times in a row, over and over again until the blaring trumpets made me flinch in real pain. After that, I never felt the same pull. Feel free to use the same method should you find yourself in a similar fix.

But through all this, I possessed a secret protection. Because I knew in the long run, after he ran out of windmills to tilt at, there was Manly Author. We both loved to read. We both had taken hits in life at an early age and understood each other's scars. He looked good in a black T-shirt. We were meant to be. After years of waiting, things seemed to be percolating just after I quit my job and was preparing to leave the country and go live on an island in the middle of the Atlantic.

It was late at night. We were driving back from a Portuguese festival. Manly had wanted to see some of the traditions I had been telling him about. About an hour from home, he told me he felt ready to date again after his divorce. I held my breath.

"Not you, of course. I know there's an attraction between us, but you're my only woman friend," he said.

I already knew this was a concern for him. He'd had a book-signing party earlier in the year, and I'd overheard one of his uncles ask, "What about her?" as I left the room.

"Nah, she's my friend," Manly had said. "You don't shit in your own chicken coop."

As I recall those words now, they do not strike me as the most romantic syllables ever spoken. But at the time what I heard was "I'm attracted to my dear friend." It was like a pretty wedding vow.

About a week after he told me he was going to date again, but not me, Manly drove me around town showing me where he got his first haircut, the site of his first job, and the house where he'd first kissed a girl. I was puzzled by the narrated tour, but Barbara said this was something men do. They like to present themselves geographically.

Physically, we were farther apart. Manly used to sit on my couch and drink tea. These days, he came in, but he stayed standing, and he talked to me from the dining room as though I were in the living room, and if I walked into the dining room, he drifted into the kitchen. It was like a waltz, only if the dancers kept a room between them. My theory was that our unspoken passion was so hard for him to resist that it required a buffer of many square feet.

It was the week I was to leave, and still nothing had happened. I had been swooning about for years, so there was no way I was going to make the first move now. I figured it had to be his turn. The only reason

I was now on my way to his house was to pick up a book he'd signed for a friend of his who was doing me a big favor. Elmano and Albertina were going to the Azores after all and would need their house for the first weeks of my stay in the Azores. I had said it was no problem, that I'd just rent a hotel room in the city. But the truth was that after the paper had taken the taxes out of my buyout check, and after I'd bought a plane ticket and a couple of cute skirts, my assets in the world totaled about $7,000.

So Manly called a friend of his who ran an organic dairy cooperative that was about half Portuguese farmers and asked him whether someone had a house in the Azores they would lend to his friend. It took him less than a day to find me lodging for those first weeks.

Arriving to fetch the autographed book, I walked straight into his kitchen. We always ended up hanging out in the kitchen.

Manly looked at me intensely. I was close enough to see his eyes. There was a gravity to them. He had waited until the last possible second, but this was it. I was sure he was going to say something I would never forget.

"Did you see Michael Jackson died?" he asked in a low rumble. "It just goes to show you, life is short."

I had seen Michael Jackson had died. Judging by news video of weeping drummers in Senegal, I'd assumed the whole world knew. Manly Author was right, of course. Life is tenuous. I had just quit my job—I was the poster child for carpe diem. Now if he would just seize the DM—that would be me.

We stared some more, and no one moved. I barely breathed. After another eternity, I started feeling self-conscious. I struggled to find my voice.

"'Thriller,'" I whispered, "was a groundbreaking video."

After a platonic back-patting man hug and the promise of a follow-up email, I went back to my car, and the city gave way to agriculture.

The sky was bleached, fields were burnt gold, railroad tracks made a *V* into a hazy horizon. I was driving north through a country song. I kept an eye on the tracks and saw some kids at a crossing putting pennies on the tracks, waiting for a good-luck smashing by a passing train. Interesting concept: being flattened into good fortune. That happens, doesn't it? You feel as if you got run over good, only to later realize you are as lucky as they come.

The fields had feathery smudges of gray green in the distance at regular intervals. Trees. They were the signal that these were family farms. Each windbreak meant a house, a porch. Usually at least two vehicles: a white pickup for the farm and an old car with good gas mileage for the drive to whatever job was paying to hold on to the land. There had once been a stand of trees for every three hundred of these acres. But in the 1950s the motto in American farming became "Get big or get out." A postwar-boom generation was groomed to expect inexpensive food, and chemicals used in World War II were turned into pesticides that helped make that possible.

I was on my way to see Manly's friend Tony. He was part of a group bent on carving out niches for smaller farms. He'd taken his farm organic, long before *organic* was a catchword, because he "didn't want to milk every damn cow in the county. I just wanted to support my family like my dad had done."

His father had emigrated from the Azores. Most of the Azoreans from Terceira were dairy farmers. I was heading to a festival at Tony's ranch, where I would meet the dairy family with the empty Terceira house and let them size me up. The festival, a mix of farm types and Bay Area eco-hipsters, was in full swing despite broiling heat. This was the place to buy local honey and sign petitions limiting the term *organic*.

A couple in hemp clothing were talking to Tony, extolling the facilities of the ranch, which often hosted weddings and family reunions.

"This could be huge. The perfect place for concerts. Only a few hours from the city," the woman said. "What's your internet strategy? You should make social networking a big part of your platform."

Tony, a lean man with bright blue eyes, wearing a cowboy hat and boots with such slouchy ease that it made it hard to imagine him in anything else, didn't say much until the couple had exhausted their words. "Yeah, we're probably already doing as well as we want to," he said. "Something my father always told me was that the trick to success is to know when you have enough and stop and appreciate it."

A woman in her late sixties with a wide smile and a sparking energy joined the group as I approached. "This is my sister Mary. She just about raised me," Tony said, introducing us, "and this is Diana-Who-Is-Off-to-the-Azores."

I handed him the book Manly had autographed for him.

"So how is our mutual friend?" Tony said.

Many years ago, my father told me I never had a thought that didn't show up on my face. He didn't mean it as a compliment. Apparently my face flashed disappointment in response to Tony's question about Manly. "Oh, honey!" said the sixty-eight-year-old Mary, grabbing my arm. "Don't worry. There's nothing a good blow job can't fix."

I was startled into honesty. "A blow job! Why, we've never even kissed!"

"Really?" said Tony. "I thought you and him were an item. I thought you two were . . . I mean, when he called . . ."

"Oh, this is serious," said Mary. "Come into my tent."

Mary's tent at the festival was set up for entertaining small children with storybooks. We sat down amid stuffed unicorns and princess headbands with long ribbons and glitter stars.

"Tell me about the first time you saw him. Take off your sunglasses. Let me see your eyes," Mary said.

I couldn't figure out why I was obeying. But I took off my sunglasses and leaned back on a plush toy dragon. "I didn't meet him. I read him," I said. "Then he read my stuff. But since then, the years put us both in the same city and left us each solo. I think I'm just wanting to make it into something that it isn't," I said. "It's nonsense."

"Love," said Mary, "is very funny. But it is never nonsense. Do you believe in love?"

Mary's expression suggested she actually expected an answer.

"Well," I said, "I do like to hear stories about it."

The Capricorn

Mary was on her third marriage. Husband Number Three, she said, was true love. She had known him in school. When she first noticed Bill, a boy with a kind smile that crinkled his whole face, she was about fourteen.

Mary said that she had loved school. She was studious, got straight As. She had a dream that if she did exceedingly well as a student, her father would let her continue beyond the age of sixteen, the minimum that state law required. Her family had come to California from the Azores in 1948, when she was six. They were at the cusp of the wave that would bring around forty thousand people from Terceira to the Central Valley. Other islands also sent large portions of their populations. There were now twice as many people of Azorean heritage in California as there were in the nine islands.

But that same frozen-in-time quality that had so enchanted me when I had first bumped into this community meant that Mary, as a young woman, had remained trapped by traditions of patriarchy and possession. For generations, landowners in the Azores had married their daughters off to the sons of other landowners, parlaying their wealth. A young woman's role was to be chaste, then chattel.

Mary's father venerated his island "old country." Later in life he would open up to a new country and new times. But Mary was the oldest, and she was raised according to tradition. She was not allowed to go on dates or to any extracurricular activities. Her father chose her future husband—the son of another family from Terceira—settling the deal with a handshake when she was thirteen.

Her plan to stay in school didn't work. When she was sixteen, the principal, Mr. McSweeney, drove out to their ranch to tell her father she was one of their best students and to plead with him to let her continue her studies. Her father said no, that the government had kept her long enough. It was time for her to learn to bake bread and sew and be a good wife. Before the marriage agreement was reached, relatives in Terceira had researched both sides of the boy's family. He came from a long line of good Catholics untouched by scandal. But, in private, he could be mean.

That summer Mary's family returned to Terceira for a family visit. Tony, a four-year-old born in the United States, was allowed to run around at will. The people in their hometown doted over "the American boy." Her younger sisters could go to the ocean and the market and even the festas as long as they were accompanied by respectable friends. Mary, however, as an engaged woman, was required to stay with her grandmother at all times.

But, she thought, she saw hope. Her father was seeing that things were not exactly the way he remembered. There were women wearing nylons and smoking in the cafés.

They met a woman professor. And from so far away, her fiancé could not lash out when she told him she wanted out. She mailed back the ring. She begged her grandfather to speak to her father about letting her stay in the Azores. He agreed.

But one day, before anything had been sorted out, her father stomped into the house. He was carrying the gold ring that her fiancé's father, a lifelong friend of her father's, had mailed back. He was angry. "A man's word is a man's word," he said. "Nothing changes that." He put the ring back on Mary's finger and walked away.

After that she didn't question her fate. At eighteen, Mary (after a physical to document her virginity) was married. A week into her honeymoon on California's picturesque Central Coast, Mary called her mother and pleaded to come home. "I can't do this," she said.

"Daughter, you made your bed and now you must lie in it," her mother said.

Inside her own head, Mary screamed she'd had nothing to do with making her bed. She stayed for twelve years. Her husband controlled her comings and goings, putting chalk marks behind the car tires. He took books out of her hands and threw them when he caught her reading.

The second husband was a kind, older man whom she said she married for her children's sake. "He didn't deserve what I did to him."

What she did was run into Bill. It was the twenty-fifth high school reunion. It was a small town, and everyone was always invited to the reunions whether they graduated or not. Mary had never gone. Even though she eventually went on to get a nursing degree, it still pained her that she hadn't finished high school. But by now, her own children grown, she figured she'd come to peace with it. It might be fun to see old friends.

She saw Bill as soon as he walked in. He was taller. He'd filled out from the pencil-thin boy she had known.

"I felt shivers up and down my arms. I had never stopped thinking of him," she said. "People always talk like love is just for teenagers. I don't know why. It isn't true. You do not become immune."

His eyes seemed to carry shadows. Mary thought she sensed pain. But his smile was still kind and crinkled his whole face. And the obedient, studious girl was long gone. Mary's marriage of convenience came with a red BMW convertible and a flashy wardrobe. She'd hidden herself behind a brazen, ballsy persona.

"Why, Bill," she said. "Do you know you've been my favorite wet dream all these years?"

She thought her outrageous joking would mask her true trembling. Bill shook his head at her, then hugged her. "Mary! My Mary," he said.

That night she told her husband she wanted a divorce, even though Bill was married. "I don't want to cheat on you, and if I ever see that man again, I will sleep with him. I feel something that I can't explain and won't deny," she said she told him.

"The next part wasn't pretty," she said. "Our story was like one of those cheap dime-store novels. I won't give you the details, but we hurt many people.

"What I will tell you is that we've been married twenty-eight years. And our love is as real as anything on this earth. It's the most important part of my life. Love absolutely exists," she said, fanning herself with a nearby glitter pom-pom. "Say, what astrological sign is this fellow you're drawn to?" she asked.

I was embarrassed that I readily knew the answer, but his birthday was near Christmas. "Capricorn," I said.

"Capricorn! That's my love. Let me tell you about Capricorns! They seem all serious and stodgy to the outside world, but wait until you get them behind closed doors! And I'm not just talking sex, but laughter too. Oh, how Bill and me just laugh and laugh. In public you would never know it, but in private my Bill is the silliest man alive. There's nothing as sexy as laughing."

There were a few things of real interest to me here. A couple pushing seventy were laughing their heads off and having sex. That was good to know considering my current romantic pace. And Capricorns are real cutups in private. In Manly's case, it was hard to imagine: I'd once watched him initiate a conversation about the apocalypse at an otherwise cheery Fourth of July barbecue.

But probably what was most important about Mary's story was that it reminded me that there's always another side to the halcyon past. The long arc of human history was slowly inching away from brutality and oppression. Traditions and hanging on to old hierarchies could be very unkind to women or children or anyone without power.

When I came out of the tent, Tony was leaning over a white ranch fence watching the sunset. It was the perfect out-west picture, right down to his one boot propped on the lower rail and his hat brim shoved back from his face. I walked over and stood by him, throwing my arms over the fence too.

"Mind a little advice?" he asked.

"I'd appreciate it," I told him.

"We've got lots of relatives over there. Some of them high-up muckety-mucks. I'll give you names and phone numbers if you want. But my advice to you is to not take me up on the offer. Don't plan too much," he said. "When you go on an adventure, just trust that you'll meet who you need to meet and hear what you need to hear because the really important stuff, you just can't plan."

PART TWO

The Shoe Repair Shop

The sun and I arrived in Terceira at the same time. As soon as I stepped out of the plane that morning, I smelled salt and flowers, and the scent seemed far more familiar than by any right it should have. I'd been here once for two and a half weeks, almost four years ago.

Elmano had told me that his village was on the north side of the island and that it would be a different experience from my stay in Angra do Heroísmo—more rural, and I couldn't depend on there always being someone nearby who could speak English. By coincidence (and the interlocking connections of Azoreans) the first house I was staying in was also in Elmano's village, and the family who had lent it to me had been neighbors to Albertina's family in Modesto.

The cabdriver who picked me up at the airport did not speak English, and when we got to the house it was locked, and there was no one in sight. I had emailed Chef that I had quit my job and was going to the Azores. But everything had been such a whirlwind that I never followed up. I hadn't stayed in touch with anyone else after initial flurries of thank-you notes, even though I had meant to. I also had not learned Portuguese, even though I had meant to. I didn't know how or where else to ask the driver to take me, so I was outside the house, in front of a cornfield, sitting on my suitcase.

I decided to walk to the village and find an internet café where I could message Frank, the home's owner, back in California. I would soon find that at this time, on this part of the island, there was no such thing. As I first came into the village's center, I saw a small café. I walked in and said, *"Bom dia, falas inglês?"* to the man behind the cash register.

A tall man drinking an espresso at the bar turned around. "You still haven't learned Portuguese?" he asked, grinning.

My brain couldn't process it. How was Chef standing in front of me?

"Do you recognize me?" I gasped, taking off my sunglasses and hat.

"I knew it was you before I turned around!" he said. "Your Portuguese is still very bad."

"But how did you know I was here?" I asked. I was delighted to see him but too stunned to do anything but stare and stutter.

"This is my village," he said. "It is you who must answer the questions."

We walked out and sat on a low wall in front of the café to talk. It faced the church and the main intersection. People kept honking, and he kept waiting and shouting greetings, so I still didn't have any answers.

"I am sorry to interrupt us to keep waving. But friendship is serious business here. It would be very bad if I missed waving to someone," he said.

Another car honked.

"That one was my mother!" he said.

"But what are you doing here?" I asked again.

"I was born here. My grandfather and my father was born here. I am the fire chief. Now you tell me what you are doing here," he said.

Within an hour of arrival, I had run into the one person I had stayed in contact with over four years, even though he knew I was coming only at some point in the summer and I only knew he lived somewhere on the island. Chef asked me whether I was still interested in the ties between the Azoreans who had left and the Azoreans who had stayed.

"Yes," I said, "I think that's what I'm interested in."

"*Bom*—good. I am teaching a computer class in Angra that you must see. I will pick you up at eight in the morning," he said. "Where do you live?"

I explained which house and that it was locked.

He looked sad. "I see," he said. "I know where we can find information."

He drove me to a house with a well-kept garden. He looked nervous knocking on the door. A petite woman answered, and when she saw him, she started crying and then stood on her tiptoes to hug him tight.

I didn't know what was happening. He gestured to me. She gave me a kiss on each cheek, as is Portuguese custom, and then gave Chef some directions (I could tell by the pointing).

In the car, Chef explained that Maria and her husband were the caretakers and they were supposed to meet me. But her husband had died of a heart attack four days earlier. Chef had been on the call, putting paddles on her husband and shocking him, trying to restart his heart. In the Azores, firefighters were also ambulance drivers and paramedics. He didn't know Maria personally, other than to recognize her, but he said that sometimes when people see a firefighter from a critical moment, they have a strong reaction. Sometimes sad, sometimes angry—even physically lashing out. It could happen even years later, when a face from that day triggers unexpected memories. He was grateful for her hug.

We picked up the key from some cousins of the family's. Pushing open the door to my temporary home, Chef laughed. "You are going to be very well acquainted with the owners of this house," he said.

The house was from the husband's side of the family, and his mother had decorated in a fiercely proud style. Every surface of every piece of furniture was filled with framed family photos. Every bit of wall space, except for the areas taken up by two tapestries of Portuguese history and a reproduction of *The Last Supper*, documented Frank's life from first

Communion to high school graduation and the lives of his children. As a reporter I'd been in many houses with the same sort of interior design. Proud Grandma is an international style.

The next morning, I met proud great-grandmothers.

Chef was teaching a computer class at a seniors' center in Angra. He walked around helping very old women open emails with photos attached. They laughed and pointed at screens showing babies and weddings and pictures of dried cod and potatoes baked Azorean style. Most of the photos looked as if they had been taken in the Central Valley.

The women themselves looked like the black-clad widows I had met at my first Azorean party at Morais's ranch. Chef told me the students were in their eighties and nineties. Most of them could not read or write. They were from an era when people went hungry and many children, especially girls, didn't go to school. But now they were clicking at keyboards and communication was visual. I sat in that computer lab watching and knew that the Azores' days separate and apart from the world were numbered.

In the village where I was staying, the garbage truck was pulled by a mule. A bread man hung bags of fresh rolls powdered with white flour on my door each morning. The fish man came by in the afternoons—and if the women hadn't seen a fishing boat heading to the docks in the past hour, they wouldn't buy the fish.

Internet was hard to find. I would write letters by hand, then go to the computer lab at the fire station, type them into a big Dell computer, and send them once the computer connected through a squawk box modem. If I had emails from friends, I would print them out to read at the house, sitting on the old stone cistern looking at the cornfields and, beyond that, the sea. It wasn't that different from picking up letters at a post office.

Writing (and taking the occasional snapshot) still seemed to me to be the most powerful human invention. The letters carried my friends to me over space and time and delivered them with full, rich clarity. Jack Moody sent me a photo of himself and a very big steelhead on the Umpqua River in Oregon. "If you were here, you would say this fish was 'SOOOO AMAZING!!!'" he wrote, teasing me from four thousand miles away.

Barbara, the journalist, knowing that I could barely call up news sites on a ragged internet connection, sent me choice articles, including one about the two eight-year-olds arrested for burglary in Fresno. They had crawled through the doggy doors of two homes. In one home, they took about $500. In the other, they left with a puppy. They got caught when one crawled back through one of the doggy doors to retrieve a walkie-talkie. And people thought they could live without a local paper?

(Barbara also said that on a spa day with her foothills cousins, they had talked her into painting her toenails cherry red with big white daisies that had immediately smudged, and she had to wear closed-toe shoes and it was 104 out, making me very grateful that I had escaped Central Valley heat.)

From Jeanne's letters I got the feeling that she and Bobby, her husband of forever, were having a squabbly summer because whatever Azorean phenomenon I wrote about, Jeanne would write back that it reminded her of Bobby. Volcanoes? Tall, dark, and waiting to explode, just like Bobby. Cobblestone streets? Antiquated, just like Bobby. I knew they would make up soon; they always did. Their only fight that ever lasted was when Bobby wouldn't let Jeanne sing with his band. He felt she couldn't carry a tune. She strongly disagreed. It reminded me of an *I Love Lucy* episode. No, I cannot tell you who was right. I value my friendships.

Bobby was an old-school jazz guy. I thought of him sometimes when I was walking down the village's main road because there was a musicality to the place. Up on the roofs, men slapped handmade ceramic tiles in place: *clink, clink, clink*. Cows mooed. The breeze whistled through cornfields like brushes on a snare, women swept porches—*swish*-pause-*swish*—and there was always behind everything the thrum of the ocean. The entire village was a riff.

I'd arrived earlier in the season, before summer's bright blue skies and the influx of the diaspora. The mornings were gray, and the afternoons a powdery silver. In California we called this June Gloom, but I liked the day taking its time kicking off the covers.

There was a little mountain (or big hill, or ancient volcano splatter cone if you want to get geological) behind the village, next to the sea. The land had once belonged to Elmano's grandfather. It was one of his uncles I'd sometimes see driving through the fields.

Every day I'd follow the long dirt trail through the cornfields and cow pastures and up to the top. On my way I'd cut down a side trail to greet a brown cow in a stone barn in two languages: "*Bom dia vaca.* How now, brown cow?" On this side trip I often got dive-bombed by a gull. There must have been a nest. The gull would drop and seem to be flying right at me, swoop over my head, and come back the other way. The inconsistencies of attack made it more exciting.

Other than angry gulls or a bull, there was no wildlife danger—not one species of poisonous snake or marauding predator on the islands. Indeed, the only animal believed to be endemic to the Azores was a bat.

At the top of the *pico* was a tall, white monument topped with a cross and blue shields commemorating some this or that, but it was hardly the point. From the top, the sea cliffs dropped straight down. Below was water so clear that on some days I could see multicolored rocks many feet below the surface. On other days it was bright turquoise froth. From this perch I could see checkerboard fields of greens and the villages along the coast in both directions, and I could wave at the house where I was staying and at Elmano's house, where I would spend the bulk of the summer.

In the afternoons I dutifully studied immigration charts and read up on volcanology and Azorean social structures because I had a vague notion that I would write a book someday, and I thought that was what someone writing a book might do. Of course, other than Manly Author, I knew no one personally who had written a book. You can see what little I have made of my research.

In the evenings I walked down to the one café in the village. I wanted to hear stories, and this was where people gathered to tell them, and if there is anything a storytelling crowd likes, it is an audience. I gathered that every Azorean summer eventually ends up with a name: the Summer Old Mateus Fell in Love (But It Ended Badly), the Summer of the Divorces, the Summer of the Canadian Girl. The last one was my favorite because it seemed as if half the village had taken part in the hijinks.

Miguel Carlos, who worked with cows, and a Canadian girl, a successful PR executive, had fallen madly in love even though she didn't speak Portuguese and he didn't speak English. They would play soccer and laugh and laugh. They walked down the street, waving their arms and miming to each other. The village decided that, as ludicrous as it was, they seemed genuinely in love. And who can explain love, anyway?

At the end of the summer, she vowed to quit her job, pack her belongings, and come back from Canada to be his wife. But after she left, Miguel Carlos decided he wasn't good enough for her and stopped calling to play her music on his guitar and speak English phrases his friends had written down for him. The Canadian girl, frantic with worry, called all his friends searching for him. He begged them to tell her he was in the hospital. They set up a fake phone number, and his friends took turns pretending to be nurses who didn't understand English. They thought that Miguel Carlos would regain his courage.

Eventually, one of his friends had to end the relationship with the Canadian girl for Miguel Carlos (since you can't mime a breakup over a telephone). She married a doctor and never went back to Terceira. He was drunk for one year straight but eventually married the schoolmate he'd loved as a child.

I told Chef how much I liked hearing the stories.

"Be careful," he said. "Or they'll turn you into 'the Summer of the *Americana.*'"

Chef could also tell a tale. This was before the height of the bullfight season, when firefighters were three times busier rushing people to the hospital, so he had time to talk between calls. I most liked hearing about his grandfather's shoe repair shop. Chef had been painfully shy as a child, although there were few signs of it now. His favorite place had been his grandfather's shop, where from a very young age he played with knives and hammers and matches and quietly listened to the shop's regulars.

There was Tio Miguel, who carried a walking stick and always wore the same coat, which was either brown or gray. (It was hard to tell because it was so dirty.) He delivered one-liners in a raspy voice like a growl. There was Tio Carreal, who would talk about what he had observed that day, whether it was how two people had negotiated a difference or the manner in which ants had moved their hill. Tio Morais, the richest man in the village, was also often there, but they seemed to keep him around just to make fun of him.

"If I could just get everyone in the village to pull for me, I could be the richest man in Portugal," he said one day.

"Well, if pulling will bring riches, why should I pull for you? I think I will pull for me," said Tio Carreal.

When he was a little older, Chef raced to the shoe shop with his friends after school for a game. His grandfather would put glue between their fingers. They would hold their hands up and go motionless while the glue set. Then they would see who was the strongest by who could pull their fingers apart first.

A farmer would come in with a boot that needed fixing. Chef's grandfather would stop everything he was doing, take a long look at the boot, and spend fifteen minutes explaining where he was going to cut and stitch and glue to fix it. Ladies would bring in their church shoes, and the Tios would put on their hats, sit up straight, and use better language while women were in the shop. Sometimes they talked politics, but though dictator Antonio de Oliveira Salazar was now gone, they looked over their shoulders.

"Even for me as a kid, I could still feel the phantom of Salazar," Chef told me during one of our firehouse conversations. "I'll never forget the way they lowered their voices when they talked politics." During the regime there had been spies everywhere. At the church, Chef's grandfather would point out people who had been willing to sell out their neighbors.

But for the most part, voices were not lowered at the shop, and everyone had something to say until they would run out of words. "That was my favorite part," Chef said. "There would be this silence. My grandfather would just keep working on a shoe, sewing, hammering."

The quiet would go on for a long time, and then someone would say, *"Epa!"* (a ubiquitous Terceira exclamation good for all situations). "Kind of cold today, eh?" Or, "Did you see Huberto's corn?" And then they were off again.

The alarm rang. Chef grabbed his jacket. "They had enough time to say all they had to say on a subject. Can you imagine?" he shouted as he ran off to the ambulance.

Hey, You! American Girl

I once read about a study trying to isolate what factors most brought happiness. After adjusting for health and basic necessities, researchers found it wasn't money or success or education. They narrowed it to two things: a sense of gratitude and enough sleep.

The former I felt I possessed. I was grateful for the sky, the ocean, the hydrangea bushes with their giant lavender blooms, fresh bread, wine, and friends, and that the Portuguese didn't eat dinner until nine at night. I mean, I might be positively swimming in grateful happiness if only I could get. Some. Sleep.

But horny birds were keeping me awake, night and day. Excuse me, that was indelicate. A love story like that of the *cagarros* deserves better. Let me back up.

Chef was acting as my guide to all things Azorean, pointing me to go on field trips and out to interview various people even though he and I both knew that I wasn't completely clear on my purposes for interviewing anyone. He felt that if someone like me with no ties to the Azores was so taken with the place, then there must be an inexplicable purpose at work. I didn't go out of my way to say, "Look around: volcanoes, oceans, lost in time. Who wouldn't be interested?" because I liked feeling anointed.

A couple of weeks back, he had arranged for me to camp with some researchers documenting the seabirds called cagarros. He had met them when one of the researchers needed to be rescued after falling off a cliff while looking for nests.

About 75 percent of the world's cagarros nest in the Azores. After mating and raising their young, the birds fly off in different directions but return each summer to the same nest (always near cliffs) and the same mate. In other words, the Azorean Islands, with a far-flung diaspora that returns each summer, are also home to a bird population that does the same.

But the birds were late. The researchers left and went to another island. For a while I had only Chef's descriptions. He said their calls were unlike those of any bird I had ever heard and that their mating calls filled summer nights. In my head I was already writing letters home filled with poetic descriptions of exquisite avian love songs.

Finally, cagarros arrived one village over, and a few of us drove down to watch and listen. We could hear them long before we could see them.

My impressions:

1. Loud
2. Very loud
3. Was that the sound of a bird or a braying burro?
4. If bird, related to Woody Woodpecker?

They swooped and circled and sang, "*Wa-ka-wa-ka WAH wa-ka-wa-ka WAH.*" It was a hiccupping chorus that sounded like that of giant frogs.

Chef told me that in the old days people called cagarros "devil birds" and found their cries eerie and haunting. I said that the only danger I sensed in their calls was that a person might die laughing.

About a week later, a colony of cagarros brought the party near my house. They whooped and hollered all night long. I've always been somewhat proud that I can sleep through anything. It's handy for a journalist to be able to sleep on planes and trains and all manner of automobiles. But this was different. There would be silence, and then a screeching cacophony would break out at irregular intervals. Sometimes I would give up on sleeping and just go watch the birds, their white undersides flashing as they rolled their bodies in flight. They were supposed to spend all day over the ocean and come in only at night, according to people who studied these things. But there were some who kept the party going in the daytime too. There are always a few who don't follow the rules, be they birds or otherwise.

Luckily it was time for me to move into Elmano and Albertina's two-story house. It had a balcony facing the sea, and even better, it was a half mile from cagarros central.

One afternoon, I was walking back to my new place after checking my email at the fire station. The day I'd left California, at the airport, after our moment-that-wasn't, I had typed Manly Author a note on my BlackBerry (I throw that in for historical detail) just describing the scene:

"Everyone is speaking Portuguese. The men are dressed in checkered short-sleeved farmer shirts, jeans with big belt buckles. The women favor decoration. They have long decorated fingernails, toe rings, and necklaces. They're wearing shirts in every sort of flower or animal print or bold solid turquoise. They carry overstuffed handbags."

I hadn't heard back until now. When I saw his name in my in-box, my pulse quickened. I hit Open.

He had sent back my email, adding only:

"Below is my last dispatch from you. *you must give me an update. how goes it?*"

Not a crumb of information about him, no declaration of affection finally realized in my absence. For the first time since I had reached Terceira, where I spent many hours alone walking around just looking at stuff, I felt lonely. Alone-in-the-universe lonely.

I was so lost in self-pity that at first I didn't realize that a woman in the house across the way was calling to me. Someone shouted it again. "Hey, you! American girl!" A woman with a silver pixie haircut and a martini shaker in her hand was waving me over. "Come here, come here. Would you like a drink?" she asked.

Her sister and her neighbors had told the woman, Romana, to keep an eye out for me because they saw me always walking by and figured I didn't speak Portuguese and must be lonely. Perfect timing.

She came every summer from Boston to stay a month here, in the house where she was born. She said the first thing she did when she arrived each year was to walk in and stop the clock on the kitchen wall. Her sister, Marilva, started it again after she left.

Romana put an icy gin martini in my hand in a land where drinks were served cold only at tourist joints. She was Audrey Hepburn–slender with an elegant air, even though she had her own cocktail glass in hand and a tambourine in the other and kept running out in the yard spilling gin and shaking her tambourine to scare away the birds eating her grass seed. Beyond her yard were acres of cornfields and, beyond them, the sea. In the middle of the corn was a stone *palheiro*—barn—with American, Portuguese, and Azorean flags waving high above it.

"I fly the American flag highest," she said. "I have them put up the night before I arrive. I am Portuguese *American*," she said.

It was readily apparent that Romana was a force of nature. It would take time to learn some of the reasons—for example, how she credited kickboxing during chemo treatments for having survived breast cancer—but the gale force of her personality landed immediately.

She wasn't the only returning native. Every week now another plane of emigrants arrived. The population tripled. Every weekend there was a crowded festa (or three) somewhere on the island. I still checked my email at the fire station, but Chef didn't have much time to tell me cobbler shop stories. He was always running out to take people with concussions and broken legs to the hospital. These were things that happened in the mad, drunken scrambles not to get gored by the bulls.

Romana didn't like the bullfights. One afternoon we were sitting on her wall drinking—a martini for her, gin and tonic with lots of that wonderful hard-to-come-by ice for me—and looking out over the corn. (How did watching the corn grow get such a bad rap? It's one of my favorite activities.) I mentioned there was a bullfight that evening, one of the bigger ones, and maybe we should go. It was a very serious communal passion: one of every six euros spent in Terceira was directly tied to the bullfights. Next to cows, Terceira's main industry was the festas.

"The bullfights!" exclaimed Romana in disgust. "I think I have been to about three in my life, and that was enough. They have got to be the stupidest thing ever. Needless to say, my sister *absolutely* adores them. Now, I would not want you to think she is stupid or something. She is actually a very nice, educated person.

"I am beginning to think that maybe it is the water in this village or maybe the whole of Terceira," she mused. "Maybe they should start drinking martinis—that would cure them."

That was actually one of Romana's more generous takes on some of the traditions.

One day I came in prattling about the *bodo de leite*—the milk parade. There had been a couple of floats, people throwing candy to children, decorated oxen, and people serving milk and sweet bread. It was part of a tradition that celebrated feeding everyone, letting no one go hungry. I had seen the same parade in California. I was enchanted by how faithfully the tradition had been passed down.

"It was beautiful," I said about the morning's parade.

Romana's gracefully shaped brows shot up. "What milk parade are you talking about? The one with the two *fat* brown cows . . . and they are not even milked, the glasses are filled with bottled milk? And the cars with a lot of women with dyed black hair making a lot of noise while everyone sits on the church stairs staring at God knows what? The same ones who only came to show off their outfits, nothing else? Is this the parade where the poor saint came down the street, carried by the silly priest dressed in his golden best, with his very serious face on because he is completely pissed out of his mind? Is that the parade that you saw?"

"Yes!" I said. "And I loved it."

They say we are hardest on ourselves, and maybe this includes our collective identities, because I had seen this same sort of critical take from Odie and Armen on Armenians. Before I left I had confided in them that I thought Manly Author and I might get together.

"Oh no," said Odie, "you should stay away from Armenian men. They are so Armenian!"

Armen, her Armenian husband, nodded in agreement. As proof, he offered a story about how their oldest son, Reni, a bartender in Hawaii, had jumped over the bar and started a brawl on New Year's Eve after his wife slapped a girl who called her a bitch. This was attributed to Reni's passionate Armenian nature, with no blame assigned to the rude girl or the quick-slapping wife.

I was once a cocktail waitress and witnessed many a barroom brawl. I can testify that being testosterone addled is a trait common to men of many ethnicities.

"But that sounds exciting," I said, just to egg them on.

"Weeeeell, Armenian men are protective. That's nice," Odie said. "But they never tell you you're beautiful. We women need the soft, fuzzy stuff."

Armen protested: "I told you that you were the most beautiful woman in the world the day after Arby was born." Arby, their second son, was thirty-two years old at this time.

This one did make me pause. He knew the exact day he'd last told his wife she was beautiful.

"Portuguese men will tell you you're beautiful ten times a day," I said, thinking of a flirtation on my first trip.

"Oh," said Odie. "Italian men will tell you ten times an hour! The Italians are excessive. But very, very nice."

"So, Armen," I asked, "why don't you tell Odie she's beautiful more often?"

"Do I tell the sky it's blue?" Armen said.

"See?" said Odie. "He's Armenian. They can't talk about their feelings. They just get dark and glowery."

I asked for any pluses to Armenian men.

Odie put a hand on Armen's arm. "Well, I will say this. If you have a craving for a particular kind of melon, like a certain summer melon, they'll go get it for you even at midnight. And they're very faithful."

This was more praise than Romana was willing to give to Azorean men. She was sixty-five and had a string of widowers constantly dropping by to see whether she needed anything. "Poor things, they all appear to be short-legged hamsters, but they think they are as handsome as Paul Newman and just as smart as Einstein," she said. "On top of it, they think that *all* women are in love with them because they are *so* handsome. Only their grandbabies are cute, but they are working at fattening them."

She was not impressed with her own popularity.

"Listen," she said, "when I was young, if a girl had an American passport, she was pretty and she could sing too. And it hasn't changed much."

Summer Flies

As the houseguest of two Portuguese American teachers, I was the object of curiosity. I couldn't open a book, step into the shower, or sneak a daytime nap without immediately hearing the "WOO-woo" call that announced visitors.

"Do you say *WOO-woo* in the States?" one neighbor asked me.

"No, we say *yoo-HOO,* but, um, not quite as often," I told her.

One day I heard the now familiar shout of "WOO-woo" and opened the door to find Francisco, who lived across the street, with a huge platter of *lapas.* The English translation is "limpets," but I had never heard of those either.

These sea snails are a Terceiran delicacy. Chef and his friends were infuriated by a law stating it was illegal to sell them but not for the restaurants to buy them. Which meant it was only the diver who could get busted. Chef and his friends could all dive beneath the sea for an eternity because they had been training their lungs since they were small boys. The first time he had mentioned he was going fishing, my ears had perked up.

"You have a boat?" I had asked.

"I live on an island," he had said. "The island is the boat."

When he went fishing, he just put on his diving mask, grabbed his harpoon gun, and jumped off. He didn't dive for *lapas*, though.

He liked swimming after fish. The *lapas* were for only the most patient divers. They had to be scraped off the rocks, which they clung to with a ferocious tenacity. They looked like rocks filled with translucent, jellied blobs.

People say they taste like the ocean—salty and clean. I wouldn't know. Although I could feel the censure of all my seafood-loving friends from past and present, I couldn't make myself taste one. All the pretty kale and lemon garnish in the world couldn't make them look like something I wanted to eat. I grew up vegetarian. I had to overcome a certain squeamishness to eat a grilled chicken breast—no way could I slurp a raw sea snail.

But here was Francisco, who didn't speak a word of English, offering me what I knew was an incredible gift.

I had to think fast. I gave him sad eyes. I put my hand to my heart and then explained, all by mime, that sadly I had a terrible shellfish allergy. I acted out hives and anaphylactic shock. I threw in some itching. He took the platter away to no doubt joyous recipients, and after that, whenever I walked into a restaurant, there was a murmur, heads would shake, and I would see people pantomiming scratching. Word traveled fast in Terceira. Thank goodness I liked fish, or they might have thrown me off the island.

Along with the house, Elmano and Albertina had lent me an old Opel. The sound it made was proof that *putter* is an accurate word. I liked the dear old car. I just didn't like driving it on Terceira roads. It was still like an arcade game: Ten points if you don't hit the kids riding double on the bicycle! Swerve around the donkey cart! In turn, I was a trifling obstacle to be roared around by every other car on the island.

With the newfound freedom of wheels, I picked up Romana's nine-year-old grandson, John, and drove us to the village of Biscoitos, where a labyrinth of ocean pools protected by lava rocks drew crowds. There was one pool so shallow and calm that it was the place toddlers learned to swim. Another so deep, they called it Belo Abismo—the beautiful abyss—where brave sorts dived off black lava-rock spires into the frothing water.

One day we were putt-putting down the road on our way for a swim, my shoulders hunched to my ears as another car roared by us. John patted my knee and said, "Don't worry! I'll be sixteen someday and get my driver's license."

John had come with Romana from Boston. He was visiting his cousins in Angra the day I first met his grandmother. The next day, we all met up at the Festa of Praia da Vitória, a highlight of festa season in the second-largest town in Terceira.

"This is John, or João," Romana said, giving both the English and Portuguese versions of his name.

"Or you can call me Stretch," John said, demonstrating a full split on the cobblestone street. "I do karate."

For the festa there were flags formed from colored lights stretching out into the harbor on a seawall. White twinkling lights crisscrossed all over the parade route. But the stars in the night sky competed fiercely for our attention.

John's cousins had been trying to force him to use Portuguese, and he seemed starved to chat in English. Within minutes we had discussed Portugal, Lady Gaga, his hunger to see Paris and China, and possible career plans, which included geographer, volcanologist, or underwear model ("It would be so easy, and they make really good money, and I already have muscles because I do karate, and I'm only nine.").

The parade hushed John and me too. The theme was the Atlantic. There were ethereal floats, shimmery and delicate, everything in blues and greens. Women with elaborate five-foot-high hairdos stood atop the floats, barely making it under the lights strung across the street. Folklore troupes came by twirling and singing and kicking their legs in synchronization. Seven beautiful women walked by in what must have been six-inch heels, each dressed as one of the continents, outfits replete with literary imagery. The imagination involved was secondary only to their ability to walk in those shoes on cobblestones.

"Isn't it amazing what people come up with when stuck in the middle of an ocean?" Romana whispered to me.

Romana had little interest in being "dipped and fried," as she called it. So most afternoons it was just John and me heading to the pools. He was the worst swimmer I had ever seen. "Watch, watch," he'd demand and then make a great deal of splashing but little forward motion.

After one of his splash sessions, we went to the outdoor café for ice cream. We were speaking English, since it was the only language I knew. A woman with an air of annoyance kept looking in our direction, perking her ears at our language.

"Are you from Canada?" she asked.

"California," I said.

"What do you think of the Azores?" she asked in such a way that you knew she was just waiting to tell us that she did not like it.

Now, many days in Biscoitos are beautiful, but this particular one was over-the-top. Bright blue sky, deep-purple ocean, sun-kissed skin, laughter, salt water. We were under an umbrella eating ice cream—note the perfect rhythm and charming meaning of just that sentence: we were under an umbrella eating ice cream.

"I love it here," I said.

"Really? Oh, I don't like it at all," she said. "I'm from Toronto, and this place just doesn't suit me."

John looked at her with astonishment. "What don't you like about it?" he asked.

"There isn't anything to do," she said.

She was a heavy woman with a turned-up nose. She turned it up even higher as she walked away, shaking her head at her life's many irritations.

"'There isn't anything to do'!" John said after she left, and we dissolved into laughter.

But boredom was a complaint heard from some of the emigrants and their children. It was one of the reasons the islanders sometimes disparaged the visiting relatives. The locals made fun of their loud clothes and voices and particularly the need of some of them for movie theaters and shopping malls. The most common insult was calling the wave of returning emigrants "summer flies."

Connie, a retired supervisor for a chicken-processing plant in California, heard a man at the airport throw the well-worn dig at an arriving crowd. She kept steaming about it and told a group of friends that she was going to say something the next time.

"I hear it again, even from a stranger, I'm going to say, 'Excuse me, I don't know if you are talking to me, but I'm going to tell you something, and if you are not talking to me, I'm going to tell you the same thing: it's the shit from the summer flies that these islands survived on for years.'"

The resentments stretched back decades. In the 1970s returning emigrants would arrive wearing new clothes and fling around presents of toasters and chocolate bars. Their impoverished relatives sometimes felt more resentment than gratitude, and then the American or Canadian Azoreans would feel hurt that they weren't respected and that all those countless hours working dairy or factory jobs had not bought them respect. The sniping was hard to square with the oral histories and letters I had read, full of longing between separated families. But then, the two emotions didn't cancel each other out.

One night in the café, after a soccer game that almost everyone in the village had watched, two brothers, both in their sixties, got into a fight. One had lived most of his life in Artesia, an Azorean community near Los Angeles. The other had stayed in the Azores. Both had progressed from dairy hands to landowners.

"You live in the islands. But you are not Azorean. You do not go to Mass!" exclaimed Californian Manuel to his brother. "I have more ash and salt in my blood," he said, conjuring up volcanoes and ocean.

"You have ash and salt in your head," yelled his brother João. "All you ever talk about is how big your refrigerator. How big your truck."

João's wife, Maria, tried to make peace, and it worked. "Let us all calm down and have another beer and talk of the new priest," she said. "Did his head not tilt a bit to one side? Did he just sleep badly, have a crick in his neck, or has the diocese sent us a defective priest?"

I was at the airport the day Manuel left. I saw him and João cry and hold each other tight.

John and I seldom ran out of things to do. We were very busy. Sometimes all in one day we would swim, nap on a rock, eat ice cream, and take pictures of flowers, before I met Romana for cocktail hour in the late afternoons, when the cornfields glowed and the setting sun looked huge behind the stalks and sea. We'd sit on the low rock wall with our garnished glasses, and Romana would tell me stories. The ones involving the CIA and espionage took me by surprise. I hadn't expected to hear about a little village being a hotbed of international intrigue.

In 1974 the regime founded by Salazar fell in a nonviolent revolution. It started with a military coup in Lisbon, but it was the following mass civil resistance that returned Portugal to democracy and ended its colonial wars in Africa. They called it the Carnation Revolution because after the coup, people poured into the streets to put carnations in soldiers' guns and men's lapels.

During the aftermath, Portugal's political fate was tense and unsettled. Portuguese Socialists and Communists vied for power. In the

Azores—rural, isolated, and on the average more politically conservative than the mainland—a call for independence gained momentum. The movement was partially financed by Azorean Americans who were strongly anti-communist. The underground Azores Liberation Front was centered in São Miguel, where entrepreneurs and farmers feared government interference or seizures if Portugal aligned with the Soviet Union. But Terceirans told me their main interest was keeping the American base. It had been there since World War II and was a key part of the island's economy and Terceirans' heavily American-influenced identity.

I'd been surprised during my first visit to hear people speaking Portuguese commonly switch to English when taking their leave and say, "See you later, alligator." And an entire room would answer, "After 'while, crocodile." A decidedly American catchphrase. It would be hard for the motherland to compete with such indoctrination.

The Azores Liberation Front vowed the Azores would go independent and keep the base American if Portugal went Communist. Both superpowers had a dog in the hunt. Altares suddenly had new foreign families moving to town. Chef said his grandfather and the Tios recalled giving them nicknames, depending on whether they believed them to be undercover CIA or KGB. The belief was that both the United States and Russia were looking to identify the man (or woman?) leading the movement in Terceira.

One afternoon, Romana was telling me the most engrossing story yet. It was at the height of the tension. An American couple had moved to town. The wife was beautiful and independent—riding horses, dancing with men who weren't her husband, hiking alone wherever she wanted to go. Romana, who had moved to America with her parents as a teen, had recently come back to the Azores as a bride. In both places, she had chafed at a patriarchal culture, and she became fast friends with this free-spirited woman. But the American's wildness went further than dancing. Soon there was an aggrieved group of women whose husbands she had slept with. They compared notes and grew angry.

Early in the morning, while it was still dark and many of the men were taking the cows to pasture, they went to the American woman's house and confronted her. Mostly they screamed. After they left, Romana stepped up to the woman alone. "Why did you do it?" she whispered.

The woman tipped up her chin and looked defiant. "I ride men the way I ride horses," she said. "For temporary pleasure."

Romana slapped her before she knew what she was doing.

In the middle of the night, that night, the couple left—which to Romana proved her suspicion correct: that he was CIA. She figured the dustup had threatened to expose him and they'd been ordered out in a hurry.

I didn't ask. But Romana had been with a group of hurt wives, and I wondered if it had to be personal for her to slap the woman.

I had clung to every word as she told the story, but at just about the point where the miffed wives were on the march, Romana had inadvertently switched to Portuguese.

"Romana, you stopped speaking English. I can't understand you!" I said, like someone who had accidentally changed the television station at the good part.

Her nephew Tiago was in a nearby hammock. "Oh, that's nothing. One more martini and she'll be speaking Italian," he said.

I thought he was joking. But that also happened a couple of times during the summer.

Each village threw its own festa each year. When it was finally our village's turn, Romana and John were off in Angra. Chef was away too. On top of being a fire chief and a computer teacher and a harpoon fisherman, he was in the band Ti-Notas. They blended traditional island songs with their own lyrics and music. They had the Azorean hit song of the summer. The way you could tell this was that every time a young person's phone rang, the tone was their happy, nonsensical song, and the band was being asked to play festas all over the archipelago. Chef was on the island of Pico to play a concert.

That exhausted my social circle. But Romana's sister, Marilva, who spoke no English, invited me to the parade with her. She said something about *bandeiras*—flags. With my limited vocabulary and friendship with Chef, I heard *bombeiros*—firefighters. She stretched out her hands in front of her and moved them up and down. I interpreted this as a firehouse.

Dear God, they're going to start a fire at the opening ceremony, I thought. *Is a rampaging bull not enough?*

But it turned out she was pantomiming a marching band with flags and clarinets.

The night of the parade, the village's small band came first. There were two tuba players. I recognized Chef's father on the snare drum. He had the same build as Chef—all legs and arms. They were followed by the Biscoitos equivalent of Boy Scouts playing drums and wearing kerchiefs.

A moment of silence and then the firehouse's contribution: all the fire trucks and ambulances roared down the street with their sirens blaring. This assault on the eardrums was followed by every motorcycle and ATV in town adding their roaring engines to the show. They weren't decorated, just loud. At the end of the street, the whole collection turned around and came back the other way: band, drums, sirens, exhaust pipes.

When Romana returned, I couldn't wait to describe to her the village parade.

She said that was nothing—the year before, the *bombeiros* had staged a theatrical production in which they had rescued a pretend victim of smoke inhalation from a balcony. The pretend victim was heavy, and according to Romana, it had taken the firefighters a very long time to get the stretcher hoisted. She said the crowd had sat in rapt attention while the men heaved and stumbled.

When Chef returned, I told him about the siren brigade.

"I told them not to do that!" he said.

I then said, with a laugh, that I had also heard about the slow hoist at last year's parade. Chef's jaw set. This he did not find funny. "That was very educational. It's important for the community to see what we do," he said. "Also, I hurt my shoulder."

Mrs. Cardoso

Mrs. Cardoso, one of the town's most notable citizens, arrived for her yearly visit. One blue-skied morning, I was getting ready to go pay my respects. Elmano called from California to say hello and check on the house. I told him where I was headed.

"Have you met Mrs. Cardoso?" he asked in a tone that several others had used when asking me the same question. I felt warned, but I didn't know about what.

I chose a skirt to wear and even ironed it. I went outside and picked a bouquet of poofy blue hydrangeas from Elmano and Albertina's hedges, tying them with a ribbon off a box of Dona Amélia pastries.

When Mrs. Cardoso opened the door, she waved me in with a flourish. She had beauty-parlor hair and a floral housecoat. She looked me over and commented that I was a very drab dresser. She herself liked color, she said. Also, she was surprised a woman my age would wear a short skirt. "The knees don't lie," she said.

In her youth, Mrs. Cardoso—according to Mrs. Cardoso—was a great beauty, a claim that the photos of her beautiful grandchildren would seem to support as we toured the family archives hanging on the walls. She told me that no man had ever loved a woman the way that her dear departed husband had loved her and that her son was almost as handsome as her husband had been. She hoped her daughter-in-law realized her good fortune in such a catch.

We then sat on opposing couches. Mrs. Cardoso told me she was going to have her house's exterior painted.

"Oh yes," I told her. "I've noticed all the painting going on in the village with everyone getting ready for the festa."

"Oh, this is different. I use *American* paint," she said.

En garde.

"I hear you're friends with the fire chief," she demanded. "Do you know about his brother? A *seven-month* baby."

I did know Chef's family history. His grandmother, the wife of the thin cobbler, had been a huge woman with a booming laugh. One of her favorite things was to lie still and pretend she was dead, and then when Chef and his friends crept near, she would spring up and send them scattering. (The worst part of his childhood was when she died and he could not believe that she wasn't just pretending.)

She liked to tell Chef and his older brother the story of their father and mother. When their father first came around her daughter, she told them, she watched him like a hawk—and she would swivel her head, demonstrating her tracking him with laser focus. But then one day she looked away for not five minutes and—they knew the words like those of a fairy tale—"The devil impregnated my beautiful daughter! Just like that! Not even five minutes!"

Later, when Chef and his brother went to school, kids tried to tease his brother, telling him they had heard his parents weren't married when they conceived him. His brother had no idea why they thought this should bother him. He laughed and said, "I know! My father, that devil. Less than five minutes!"

I repeated the story and looked at Mrs. Cardoso with eyes of wide feigned innocence. "Isn't that amazing, that a woman in that day and age managed to outmaneuver small-minded gossips?" I asked.

Mrs. Cardoso stared me down, silently taking some sort of measure. It seemed a détente might have been reached. She invited me to see her wardrobe choices for her stay.

We walked into the bedroom, and there were three empty suitcases and clothes stacked on the bed. She held up outfits—each shirt (with coordinating pants, sandals, and bag) was more colorful, appliquéd, and patterned than the last. Each item came with an announcement of a price tag: "My granddaughter paid sixty-eight dollars for this," she said, waving a blue-fringed bucket bag.

Then the grand finale. From a garment bag with furtive flair she pulled out a dress as flashy as an ice dancing costume. It was black, but sequins burst in star patterns over one shoulder. Glittering stitched swirls crawled the length. The hem had baubles. "Just in case—you know," she said.

I did not know.

"In case someone dies while I'm here. God forbid," she said, rather wistfully packing the dress away.

By the end of that summer, I would realize how Mrs. Cardoso's generation had come back, flaunting American dollars, desperate for a salve of respect from the ache of being outsiders, immigrants in California. They had felt forced to leave the Azores by economic conditions and had held fiercely to their vows of "I'll come back someday and show you," now only to be seen by some as a yearly invasion of country-bumpkin relatives.

There was a day, near the end of my stay, when the light had turned autumnal gold, glinting off corn that had grown five feet higher since the day I'd first met Mrs. Cardoso. I was walking through the village, feeling something inside my chest—an expanding ache—and wondered whether it was early-stage *saudade*. The bells of the village church rang, the heavy wood doors opened, and congregants from a funeral spilled out. I grabbed an ice cream from the nearby snack bar, sat on a low seawall across from the church, and knew as sure as sugar (as the Portuguese say) that Mrs. Cardoso had to be somewhere in that church in her resplendent dress.

She'd been a teenager, the daughter of crushing poverty, when she married an older man and moved to a dairy farm in California where people had not always been kind. I sat right there and waited for a glimpse of Mrs. Cardoso returning to the Azores in all her glory.

Mysteries

It was very early in the morning. But there it was: "WOO-woo! WOO-woo!"

The night before, I had been at one of the festas until three in the morning (I left a bit early by Azorean standards). I stumbled to the door disheveled and half asleep. It was Romana, dressed and animated, and her sister waiting in the car.

"C'mon," Romana said, grabbing my hands and pulling. "We're going to another village to the best butcher for Marilva to get meat for the *alcatra*"—a traditional Azorean dish of meat cooked in a clay pot—"and it's beautiful along the way."

"I'm not dressed," I pointed out, stating the obvious. "I was in bed. Like everyone should be."

"Who cares? Come like that," she said, still pulling.

Luckily I was bigger, or I would have been forced out the door in only a T-shirt without shoes or brushing my teeth. I was sorely tempted to go back to bed. But I'd long ago learned "Why not?" is the best answer to "Let's go" and also that I was no match for the Romanas of this world.

The sky was bright poster-paint blue, and the sun was shining. We careened around climbing roads that went up, up, up with endless views of the sea. In one village, we stopped to visit cousins of Romana and Marilva's and ate grapes we'd picked off the trellis in the courtyard. Back on the road, we passed a house with pumpkin vines growing down the wall and each pumpkin sitting on its own little shelf.

"Which came first?" Romana wondered aloud. "The pumpkins or the shelves?"

I wanted to know what would happen when the pumpkins got bigger than their little ledges.

Romana swung around, parked the car, and went up to ask. She had what seemed to be a long chat with the farmer who opened the door. But when she got back in the door, she delivered the answer succinctly.

"He said life is better with mystery."

Chef wanted me to see the strides Terceira was making toward sustainable ecotourism and mapped out a day of research.

It was early in the morning, and we were on our way to the first stop, a mountaintop lagoon. It was a place, he said, that would be a gift to visitors from all over the world. One of the early tourism signs had recently been installed there.

I asked Chef whether he went to the lagoon often. He said he hadn't been there since he was a teenager. In answer to my raised eyebrow, he said that all over the world, people pay no attention to wonders if they are in their backyard and if it is a long walk.

We rode his quad up to the trailhead. The sign was new. It was large. The directions were in both Portuguese and English. They were useless. It has been a while, and the sign has since been replaced with a glossier, more coherent version, so I am making up the exact wording, but I am in no way exaggerating the gist of the content:

"Travel one quarter mile to the Azorean laurel tree that is taller than all the others except for one, turn right, when the trail splits, take the one that is initially smaller until it crosses the larger and becomes the bigger of the two. Climb off trail for three hundred feet until you see a big rock next to a smaller rock that is near the beginning of the true trail that is a tunnel."

"Hmm," said Chef. "They have written an interesting novel, but I think we will use my memory."

We passed many rocks larger than smaller rocks and eventually found a trail that really was a tunnel. A footpath barely wider than my hiking boot cut through dense, dark-green shrubs. We started climbing. White wisps of Atlantic fog swirled around us. Chef told me we were in a cloud forest. I thought he was waxing poetic, but it is the name of a specific ecosystem. Known in the islands as *laurisilva*, these ancient forests drink in mists and create a cool, moist habitat for many unique plants and creatures. Cloud forests once covered much of ancient Earth but now make up about 1 percent of global woodlands and are one of the ecosystems most vulnerable to climate change.

Chef was scouting ahead, and with the twists in the trail and the mists, it felt as if I was alone on the mountain. The trees and plants around me were remnants of the era just after dinosaurs disappeared. A favorite English phrase of Chef's (and much of Terceira's) was "Out of this world." They were the first words that came to my mind on this otherworldly mountainside of dripping green. But I dismissed the sentiment as inaccurate. This place didn't feel separate but rather at the very heart of things. It was as though I had stumbled onto a secret control room.

Maybe I had. I was walking through a glimpse of preglacier Europe. There were trees and grasses and birds around me that existed nowhere else on the planet. Who knew what secrets of adaptation and survival they held?

The lagoon—a volcano crater—was dark, glimpsed through mists. I asked Chef whether it was all right to go swimming, even though I wasn't sure I wanted to. He said that if I was wearing sunscreen, I should not go in because I'd put chemicals into a fragile body of water. I didn't go in. I have red hair—I am always wearing sunscreen. Chef didn't go in either. He didn't see the use in swimming anywhere other than in the ocean.

Climbing down, I carefully picked each step, fighting the steepness. I was doing it all wrong, Chef said. Watch him. Learn. He took giant strides, almost leaps, letting gravity carry him. He bounded around a bend, and the momentum took him right into a dirt bank. A full-on "Wile E. Coyote foiled by Road Runner" splat. I knew he was OK because he first looked over each shoulder to see whether I had seen. I tried to back up around the corner to save him embarrassment, but he saw me trying to hide that I saw him, and we both laughed.

"As you can see, this is a very efficient way of moving," Chef said. "It's how professional firefighters do it."

Our next stop was Terceira's surest shot for a tourist attraction: Algar do Carvão, probably the only known place in the world where you can walk inside the cone of a volcano. There was an initial explosion some three thousand two hundred years ago, and then two thousand years ago another eruption at the same site spewed molten lava inside the mountain. When the lava drained, it left chambers whose rock walls were as varied in colors of bronzes and golds as the cloak of the lover in the Gustav Klimt painting *The Kiss*.

We paid our six euros to *Os Montanheiros* (The Mountaineers), who run the site. The man working the counter told me the group first explored the cavern in 1963 when a farmer's cows had gone missing. The search party discovered the open mouth of the volcano. The mountaineers lowered a man on a chair tied to ropes down the pitch-black hole. His lantern showed the cows' bodies at the bottom of the three-hundred-foot pit.

At the beginning of the exhibit and throughout the self-guided tour were new signs paid for by the Azorean regional government to serve Terceira's awaited tourists. The signs had a Portuguese flag with the words *Você está aqui* across from it. Beneath that there was a British flag and across from it, "You are here." Beneath that, an American flag and across from it, "You are here." Beneath that, a Canadian flag and . . . well, you get how each country was individually served.

We went through a long cement tunnel with eerie lighting from electric torches. Opening the glass door to the cavern, I felt a blast of chilled air and walked inside a volcano. Stone steps led down, down, down, getting slicker with moisture until they reached a lake at the bottom. The walls dripped stalactites, formed by silicic acid deposits, rare things in this part of the world. They seemed to be in motion, growing longer before my eyes. But the stalactites only grow between one-half and two centimeters every century.

Looking up through the interior of a cone flocked vivid green by spongy, lacy, dense mosses, I could see the sky through the volcano's opening. Tree branches jutted partly across the circle of sky.

"See those branches?" Chef asked. "They look so different from this perspective."

When Chef was a boy, the volcano's existence was known, but there was no visitor's entrance, no admission booth. One day Chef and his regular group of pals (many of the same ones he still hung around with) decided to go looking for the volcano. With a rough map and bushwhacking their way, they found the mouth. They drew straws to see who would lie on the branch looking down while the others held their heels.

Chef lost (or won in his opinion). The then-skinny boy lay on those slender branches and peered down into the deep volcanic cavern.

Even though it made me shudder to think how easily he could have met the unfortunate fate of the farmer's cows, it was also exciting to think that a short time ago, there had been such unregulated adventures to be had.

Chef was contemplating going to university. He loved his job, especially when it was search and rescue and he could do the grown-up version of stretching across the mouth of a volcano. But firefighters' bodies age. They can't carry stretchers and climb cliffs forever. If he did get hurt, he wouldn't be able to move into a higher level of management without a college degree, and he had a family to support.

He was also moved by curiosity about himself. Chef read a lot, and he internalized the wisdom of his grandfather. It had long been Chef's opinion that he was smarter than the college graduates running the show. But how would he fare playing on their field? Would it change him?

Chef, the Azores' most loyal advocate, was at the same crossroads as the islands themselves—wanting to compete in the larger world but wanting to protect his essence and remain unchanged.

He said the Azores, especially with the American base scaling down, needed the cash tourism could bring in. When Portugal joined the European Union, part of the deal was that the Azores would produce less milk but receive financial support to grow a hospitality industry. The ten-year plan for Terceira was to cater to eco- and adventure tourists who would stay mostly in small rural guesthouses. There would be no cheap flights or discounted rooms in big hotels—there was no desire for mass tourism. São Miguel, the chain's biggest island, got the bulk of visitors, and that was fine with most everyone on the other eight islands. The general sentiment boiled down to "You can keep them." This was before the European Debt Crisis, when desperation set off a fight over loosening regulations.

Chef made me promise that if he did go to university and I saw it changing him, I had to say something.

It's such a pretty fantasy that we can let in the world and stay the same.

The Manly Author

There is a love more sensuous, more perfect, more above all the riffraff of other people's mere TV-binge-watching, household-tasks ordinary love than any other. It offers spiritual understanding and untold erotic possibilities.

I am speaking, of course, of unrequited passion.

For so long I had carried the warm glow of knowing that Manly and I were destined for rich fulfillment (in the form of the man and woman who would emerge once we realized that we were Meant for Each Other and transformed into burnished, shining versions of ourselves). But it was all suddenly at risk. We were actually considering getting together.

It started with emails, both of us writing late at night. And, well, the written word was our thing. But then came the phone calls. And he didn't know his lines! I didn't either! None of it was going according to the script I had spent so long perfecting. Even the erotic part. In my mind such things had unfolded with a steamy certitude. But our conversations about pairing were as scintillating as a bank merger. I protested. Why were we so formal? Did he find it odd we had never mentioned sex?

At that point in the conversation, we were discussing whether he should pick me up at the airport upon my return. He said he wasn't sure what that had to do with sex. Was I suggesting we do it in the car?

Hmm, I thought, *a chance to spice things up.*

"Yes," I said.

"That wouldn't work. Your legs are too long," he said.

He was probably joking. I missed the joke. Because whenever I wore my favorite boots, he pointed out that they made me a little taller than him. I told him I knew my being tall was a problem for him but that he wasn't that short. (It didn't come out quite the way I had meant it.) None of this was the "Oh, babys" I had fantasized.

No problem. I would rewrite. Now I walked around chuckling to myself how after our first night of amazing passion, we would laugh about this awkward start.

Except now even our emails were fraught. If love letters were a form of optimism, then these were hardly love letters.

He kept asking the same questions. What if it didn't work out? How did we get back to being friends? I would then pounce on his wobbling: "So your heart isn't in this? You expect to go straight back to being buddies?"

My dad would have proclaimed the both of us jumpier than porcupines in a balloon factory. Which brings me to my Fiesta Village Waterslide Theory.

The Fiesta Village Waterslide Theory

One of my first jobs was at the Fiesta Village Waterpark. My job there was to work on my tan while saying, "Go." *Pause.* "Go." *Pause.* This was to ensure that the kid in front got out of the pool before the next kid down the slide landed on his head.

The only holdup in this process was the kid who would get to the top of the slide and just stand there.

"Go," I would say.

But go the child would not.

> I wasn't unsympathetic. I myself was afraid of heights. I had jumped off the high dive just once—to get the life-saving certificate that allowed me to have a job where I worked on the tan that in later years left me speckled and forever wearing a hat. I got a little dizzy climbing up to my waterslide post.
>
> But the climb back down the ladder for children who wouldn't jump was torturous defeat. I always waited as long as possible before guiding their descent one step at a time.
>
> The Fiesta Waterslide Theory holds that once you get to the top of the waterslide, you have to jump, or it's a sad trudge down.

On the other hand, none of it seemed quite real with Manly and me, and I did have an overactive imagination.

Armen would have said, "This is wrong thinking!" about my water-slide wisdom and told me there's a Persian proverb that says it's never too late to turn back from the wrong direction.

My dad would have said, "Sometimes that dog just won't hunt." And if Manly and I were those pathetic kids, maybe it was better to carefully choose our steps back down to the bottom than getting thrown over, chlorinated water going up our noses.

It turned out to be not my choice to make.

A woman in Fresno was cooking up bowls of potato salad and buying chocolate cake.

"She keeps coming by here. I don't invite her," Manly told me over the phone.

I realized the moment had come. He was obviously working up to telling me that this pushy woman had made him realize that I was different from all the others. The one. I walked up to the balcony so I would have a beautiful view of the sea for the conversation that would dispel my doubts. And. Change. Everything. Forever.

"Diana," he rumbled. "She showed up here today with a picnic and said she wasn't taking no for an answer. And I realized it's just so much simpler than us."

For the first time in a long time, we talked. Really talked—me and the wounded, witty friend I actually knew. The guy who had little to do with my gauzy, romantic daydreams and probably never would.

I got off the phone.

"'Thriller,'" I whispered to the ocean, "was a very groundbreaking video."

It was getting close to time for Romana and John to go home. The corn was so tall now that you could barely see Romana's trio of flags from the road. The light kept shifting to a burnt gold.

One afternoon at the firehouse, Chef was making schedules, I was writing a letter to Odie and Armen, and Chef's band member Mox, a renewable energy engineer, was fixing a computer. It was quiet and we were all engaged in our own tasks, when some subtle movement of cloud or sun tinted the office with a warm glow. Mox looked out the window and said, "Look, Graciosa." The island across the way that was visible only on some days was reflecting light as if wrapped in foil.

I had music on my computer, and the song playing happened to be "Hallelujah" by Leonard Cohen. Mox started singing along. Chef harmonized:

> There's a blaze of light in every word.
> It doesn't matter which you heard.
> The holy or the broken Hallelujah.

Here's to Nothing

It was John and Romana's last night in Terceira. I walked over to their house. It felt as if I was saying goodbye not just to them but to this magic sliver of time—the summer John was nine, I was lost, and Romana served martinis.

Romana was watering the grass, which had finally sprouted, and looking out at the cornfields and the sea. There was that wonderful water-hitting-grass smell. She said she was thinking about her father and her mother.

"I don't think any two people ever loved each other the way they did," she said.

Romana was married, but he lived on São Miguel Island and she lived in Boston. I knew this from John, who explained to me one day that his grandparents said marriage works best when people live in separate countries.

I told Romana I thought I might be feeling *saudade*.

"That can be happy or sad," she said. "There's no translation. Absolutely none."

She kept looking at the sea.

"I am American," she said, apropos of nothing. I knew she was talking about more than a passport. Romana worried that she had stopped being like her parents.

She had an old photo of her father in a straw hat standing on their land near the rock wall. Earlier she had put on that hat. She'd had me take a photo of her at the exact same spot. Marilva and John had held up the old photo and shouted directions to Romana and me so we could get the angle, the stance, and the background as close as possible.

"I look like him," she said when I showed her the shot on my camera screen. "He was the best man I have ever known."

Romana was standing even straighter than usual and didn't take her eyes from the sea.

"I keep coming back," Romana said. "Why? Is it to pay for my sins? When I get to heaven, the Good Lord will say, 'Oh, here comes the poor one who went to Terceira every year. She's had enough punishment—let her in, she's either simpleminded or a saint.'

"I think I just outgrew them or they outgrew me. I haven't figured that one out yet. I'm not better or worse. I just have nothing in common with the people here, and sometimes it makes me sad," she said.

John was building a scarecrow to take Romana's place protecting the grass. We propped up the scarecrow, which had a flapping jacket and even a pipe (I think John had confused scarecrows and snowmen). Romana decided we should also have a bonfire. She had one of her most diligent admirers bring over a stack of dead trees and invited the neighbors.

As the sun went down, she passed out tambourines and Mexican tourist maracas. We lit the fire. It made glorious popping sounds. We danced around the bonfire whooping and hollering, making as much joyful noise as possible.

Afterward, I stopped at the fire station. Everyone except Chef was asleep. It was past visiting hours, but I told him I needed to do something on the computer that couldn't wait. I climbed up the stairs and, in the computer glow, sent an email to Odie. I'd left some of my money with her so that when the time came that I was running out and needed to go home, I would have enough for a plane ticket. I asked her to transfer the last bit of my funds. Then I made a flight reservation for home. Not that I had anything or anyone waiting for me. But I didn't know why I was in the middle of the Atlantic either.

Chef was getting off his shift. He drove me home and came in for a beer. He knew all about my feelings for Manly. I told him what had happened.

"I don't have anything," I said. "I don't have money. I don't have a job. I don't have love. I don't have a clue about what I'm going to do next."

Chef stretched out his legs and took a long drag on the ever-present cigarette that made me worry about his health. He raised his beer.

"Here's to nothing," he said. "That's when anything can happen."

PART THREE

Get Over!

When I got back to California, I was broke.

Not just my-black-boots-are-looking-shabby-and-I-can't-afford-to-replace-them broke but should-I-pay-rent-or-eat broke.

Luckily, it was only half of the rent because Matt, the river researcher subleasing my house, was offered a job in Fresno before he finished his PhD. He put his studies on hold and took it. There was a recession, and this wasn't a time when a person turned down a job, even if he had a fiancée and a pet rabbit and a whole other apartment in Santa Barbara.

Matt saved me a lot of money on bills by

1. splitting them,
2. being a dedicated environmentalist.

We seldom turned on the air conditioner, and we hung our socks on the back porch to dry.

I didn't have time to look for a "real" job because I was too busy freelancing for the *Los Angeles Times*. It was the newspaper I had grown up with, and I had dreamed of being a *Los Angeles Times* reporter since I was a kid. I had no precocious interest in politics or world affairs. I read the newspaper for things like Column One, a regular feature on the front page, the only requirement of which was that it be good reading. It didn't have to be news per se. The stories were about quirky things all over the world or sometimes things right in front of you that you had never thought to wonder about. I think they called them human-interest stories back then, when there was a belief that most humans shared a common interest in one another.

A *Los Angeles Times* editor had called me shortly after my return from the Azores. I was sitting in front of my computer at my dining room table working on an airline magazine story about the top five this-or-thats, hoping the freelance check arrived before my unemployment benefits ran out. I was bored.

The phone rang. News was breaking near Fresno, and she wanted to hire a local freelancer to get there fast. I put on my hiking boots and grabbed a notebook and my car keys—a routine that still felt familiar.

In tiny Minkler, a Sierra foothills community about twenty miles east of Fresno, a man had gunned down three law enforcement officers. One was dead, another not expected to survive. The man was barricaded, and a gunfight with hundreds of officers was echoing through the mountains.

I was feeding information to reporter Steve Chawkins, whose byline I recognized as that of someone who wrote slyly humorous slice-of-life pieces, when he wasn't covering murderous rampages. Since I knew he was that sort of writer, I also told him about how beautiful the orchards were that time of year, how a sheepdog was trying to befriend a police officer, and how in Minkler, Mary, Charlie, Sally, and Jeff had all known one another forever. I thought he might want to write a follow-up story.

What I didn't know was that Steve knew my byline. He kept an eye on papers all over the state and had an amazing ability to never forget a name. He remembered mine from stories that he'd read two years earlier. He told his editor, Carlos Lozano, that I should write the follow-up on Minkler.

Journalism had siren-called Carlos out of Texas. He championed writers and immigrants and was a sucker for a Merle Haggard song, especially if it was about Tulare's Kern River. Carlos had long believed the agricultural Central Valley needed more of a voice in the paper. Soon I was regularly writing about life in rural California, such as the high school that lost seven recent graduates to the wars in Iraq and Afghanistan and a championship chess team of farmworkers' children in California's poorest town.

The stories had to make the front page for me to make rent. In the beginning I made $600 for a front-page story and $300 if it went inside. It bumped up as Carlos kept lobbying for me, arguing that a writer who knew the Central Valley was too valuable to let turn into a Dorothea Lange photo of malnourishment. I had my dream job—aside from that I wasn't actually employed.

I lived close to my old newspaper office, so Barbara would come over at lunch. She'd bring a Lean Cuisine and use my microwave, since she knew I was always low on groceries. She considered things to be trotting right along for me, money be damned.

"It's just a matter of time. They're going to hire you. I can feel it," she said with her trademark zeal.

I knew it wasn't true. The *Los Angeles Times* couldn't hire anyone. Five years earlier, a foulmouthed real estate billionaire named Sam Zell had bought the company that owned the paper. On his first visit to the newsroom, he stood in front of everyone and promised he had an "open kimono" policy. It was an unsettling image to many, since Sam Zell looked like a cross between Mr. Magoo and Popeye. He financed his deal to buy the paper with employee pensions, belittled and demoted those who stood up for journalistic integrity, and brought the paper to its knees. He left it in bleak, endless bankruptcy proceedings after he finished bilking it. I wasn't going to get hired because there was a hiring freeze courtesy of the Zell years. I was just temporarily living the dream. My plan was to—as Odie often advised—worry about tomorrow, tomorrow.

Then I faced a bull.

My Azorean contacts had led me to a story about the *forçados*, guys who line up like dominoes and stop a bull by letting him run into the bunch of them. There was now a generation of California-born *forçados*.

I was reporting in the town of Stevinson (population 290), standing behind the bullring wall and talking to a few of the bullfighters while the rest of their team was in the ring with a bull. There was a higher wall between the stands and me. I was facing the other direction and didn't see the bull escape the chute as he was being taken away.

The man I was talking to yelled, "Get over!"

"Get over what?" I asked.

"The wall!" a dozen men shouted at me as they leaped the wall to the stands in a split second. To my eternal amazement, I did, too. Usually jumping a tennis net seems a feat to me, but it's amazing what a person can do when a bull is loose.

That night I thought about my financially unstable situation. I wrote the metro editor a note about how I had realized while jumping over a wall in front of a bull that I really needed health insurance.

A few weeks later, my editor, Carlos, called. "Are you sitting down?" he asked.

I figured he was telling me they couldn't send a photographer up to shoot one of my stories. Again. With an exasperated sigh I plopped down on a kitchen stool.

"I am now," I said.

"You're hired," he said.

I find it to be an uncontested truth that at newspapers regardless of whatever happens at the corporate-overseers level, someone in the ranks will still find a way to get things done. Actually, I find that to be a truth about the world in general. Carlos and the editors above him had outmaneuvered the roadblocks. The other editors wanted Carlos to be the one to tell me, since he had pushed the hardest.

Carlos was in his boss's office in LA. There was a bottle of Patrón tequila on the desk. They were waiting to whoop and holler and toast.

In Fresno, I said nothing. I was frozen. They waited. Silence.

"Diana, are you there?" Carlos asked.

More silence. I couldn't even answer that one. I had wanted this since the fourth grade.

The job was a whirlwind. I was no longer just cherry-picking stories but was responsible for the whack-a-mole of covering a region.

To handle the stress, I bought a Ping-Pong table. Barbara, her husband, Bruce, and I tried to assemble it, but there were a hundred parts and almost as many pages of instructions.

The next day Moody came over to have a look. The first thing he did was rip up the instruction booklet. Then he put the thing together. He'd drop by in the afternoons for a quick game. A lot of the times he beat me. But not when we played while I was on deadline. Adrenaline gave me a really good serve.

Chuva

Here's the thing about drought.

It's not like other natural disasters that unequivocally strike. For fires, earthquakes, storms, and floods, there is a precise moment, a before and after. With drought, there's always an if. If it still hasn't rained by the end of October. If there isn't snow by February. If there's another dry year and then another one. There's not even an agreed-upon definition of drought—it's a complex mix of rainfall, economics, and politics. Especially in California, where rivers are rerouted and water is bought and sold.

Who gets hurt, who suffers, is another list of ifs. If you're poor. If you're rural. At least at first. Until it's everyone.

I was aware that we'd had a long dry spell in the Central Valley. But I was out on a different story that had nothing to do with a lack of rain when I first started noticing that something was amiss. There was even more desperation in the poorest parts of the valley. It was in pockets, a puzzling checkerboard. Families told photographer Michael Robinson Chavez and me that there was no work—their entire neighborhood had fled to other states—while a half mile down the road, it was business as usual, ranch houses with green lawns and well-watered fields churning out profits.

Our colleagues with expertise in agriculture and business told us drought wasn't showing up in the numbers. On the one hand, the

Central Valley, which stretches 450 miles from Redding to Bakersfield, with the Sierra Nevada to the east and a coastal range to the west, is probably the single most productive tract of farmland in the world. California produces almost half of all the fruits, vegetables, and nuts consumed in the United States. The Central Valley grows hundreds of crops, from almonds and artichokes to pistachios and peaches. At certain times of the year, almost every head of lettuce in the country comes from California. The state's agricultural industry dwarfs that of any other state.

But despite all this, agriculture accounts for less than 2 percent of California's economy, a speck against Hollywood and Silicon Valley. What's more, the fields were still producing—large growers were just digging deeper wells or were first in line for water allotments. Food prices had not risen significantly. The first people to get hurt by the drought were statistically insignificant.

We didn't care about the numbers. We were seeing the faces. We were hearing the panicked voices.

Michael would drive from LA, stay in a hotel in Porterville, and get up at three in the morning to be with the farmworkers looking, with little hope, for day jobs. There weren't any. The smaller farmers who didn't have water rights had left fields fallow. It would have cost them money to grow crops with the rising price of water.

I would stay up many nights writing the stories for Column One. I kept a stack of John Steinbeck paperbacks on the table for inspiration. For Christmas, the Column One editor Kari Howard gave me a first edition hardcover copy of *The Grapes of Wrath*, just in case I didn't already feel enough pressure.

The drought kept getting worse. School enrollment in farm-town schools was dropping. Michael and I spent two days at an elementary school where there were more kids waiting in line with their families for food boxes for the road than there were left in classes. Still, evening after evening, I left an area where every hope of survival was on rain and returned to a comfortably unaware neighborhood of green lawns and sprinklers on timers. It was an hour-and-a-half drive to the areas I was writing about, but neighbors would ask me what was going on out there as if I'd returned from a different country.

I've always done my best thinking in the shower, a common trait, I believe, among writers. But I could no longer write in my head while watching water go down the drain. I knew that in the outlying areas, people kept a bucket in their shower to catch the leftover water to put on any garden plants still alive.

Slowly but unrelentingly, the suffering moved from undocumented workers to small farmers to entire towns. In the Central Valley the very land was sinking as farmers pumped water out of depleted aquifers. The air was thick with pollution. Without rain to scrub the sky, chemical-laced particles tinted it a rusty gray. In the evenings there was a dark charcoal strip across the horizon.

I always had a headache. I had to choose between staying inside and going for a bike ride that would make me worry about that burning feeling in my chest.

My dog, Murphy, was two years old at this time. He had been a notoriously unmanageable puppy, bent on destruction. Everyone assured me he would calm down when he turned two. This did not happen (until he was three, and suddenly some switch flipped and he was the very definition of mellow). But at two, the only way to live semipeacefully with Murphy was to throw him a ball until my arm felt as if it would fall off. I worried, though, that it wasn't good for him to be running outside. You know it's bad when you think breathing the air might be worse than not exercising for an unruly Labrador. You worry, knowing that people are in the same quandary with their children.

One August weekend, I was on my way to the Central Coast to meet my friend Shellee for a break. I couldn't wait to let Murphy chase seagulls in ocean air. Maybe I would run in zigzags behind him and the birds and breathe, breathe, breathe.

There was a fire burning in the Sierra that was growing and had officials worried. But since the drought, there was always a fire burning in the Sierra that was growing and had officials worried. I wrote a news brief, filed it, and threw a duffel bag in the car, for once lugging shorts and flip-flops instead of a field reporter's hiking boots and fire gear.

An hour later, I got a call from an editor and turned around. The Rim Fire was exploding. I dropped off Murphy with a neighbor, ran into my house, and grabbed the gear I had left behind.

It was the first time, firefighters said, that they had fought a fire they weren't sure they could put out. The trees and brush were so dry and flammable, the air so dry and hot. Base camp, always a safe spot chosen for resting and managing operations, was evacuated and burned over. Twice.

Weeks after the main Rim Fire fight (it would smolder for months), I learned that a risky backfire operation, which neither the press nor higher-up fire officials knew about, had saved a grove of giant sequoias that were among the oldest living things on earth. If the last-ditch dare had failed, the fire line could have likely jumped the Merced River and roared into the famed Yosemite Valley.

The more slowly unfolding disasters were just as awful. In parts of California, cattle and horses were starving. There was no grass for grazing.

Everyday life changed. Parents taught their children that if they didn't drink their whole glass of water to pour the rest into the dog's bowl. A man used his leftover dishwater to try to keep his dead wife's favorite rosebush alive.

Yards and playgrounds and parks were brown. Some lakes and rivers were low and some were gone. I got the nickname Ms. Droughtfire, and it stuck because drought and fire were now the only things I wrote about.

On the weekends, to get away from thinking about environmental disaster, I liked to go up to the highest elevations, where it was cool and the air was better. Moody, still down the street, would swing by in his white pickup truck to get Murphy and me, and we'd drive up into the

Sierra until we reached green trees and lakes. Moody and I had been hiking together for years and had our favorite routes.

I very clearly remember the first weekend that I had a premonition of how much worse the drought might get because that was also the hike of the Famous Black Mold Incident.

The Famous Black Mold Incident

A friend of mine in Los Angeles had mentioned she had a weakness for silver-haired men with blue eyes. Moody wasn't my type (i.e., someone who made me feel as if he noticed me), but I was aware that objectively speaking he was handsome: his hair was going silver and he had blue eyes.

I was going to broach setting him up. I was also going to fill up a second water bottle. But Moody was impatient and said he had a backup big enough for both of us.

We got lost. It was his idea to go off-trail. We ended up on a sun-blasted incline, having to push Murphy up over boulders. I ran out of water. We finally got to the lake and sat on a log.

"Hand over your water," I said. I took a swig and wrinkled my nose.

"This tastes weird," I said.

Moody was holding the cap. He looked at it and nonchalantly said, "Oh, that must be why." It was covered with *black mold.*

I choked, fighting back a gag reflex.

Moody said, "Oh, Marcum, don't overreact. You're always so dramatic."

I said, "It's black mold—it's poison!"

"Oh, brother," he said. "That's only if you breathe it."

I decided he was not a man I could send to LA to meet a sophisticated woman. Moody was not dating material. Which was fine by him. He just wanted to tromp around the forest and read his *National Geographic* magazines and be left alone.

After I calmed down about him poisoning me, we found a place to fill my water bottle and kept hiking to a higher lake. He was a good companion for a moment like this because he really looked at things. He had a way of talking with his eyes more than words. I usually favor words, but in this case, as we kept noticing unsettling things, eyes worked better. It was too intangible for sentences.

We went by the recreational lake below with its docks on dry land. That was part of the state's system that moved water here and there and bought and sold it. That we commented on.

But when we reached one of our favorite natural lakes, a granite bowl that had filled with melted glaciers eons ago, we were quiet. We had never seen the water level drop before. Moody nodded at one red flower with a little spot of snow in front of it. I remembered him taking a photo there of deep snow in late July a couple of years back. That spot was always in the shade.

We started patting bark, rolling pine needles in our fingers. There were several smaller wildfires burning, and we kept sniffing the air. We were by no means scientists or naturalists; we just knew that it was even worse than we'd realized.

If it's true that animals have a sixth sense about natural disasters, it didn't apply to Murphy and drought. He jumped into the lake and swam in circles and barked and yelped in joy, and I was offended when Moody called my dog a jackass.

I talked to scientists, and they said there were no guarantees that the drought would ever end or, if it did, that the next one wouldn't be worse. They said this was very likely part of a bigger change in the climate, not just strange weather.

Driving in town one day, I saw a car with a bumper sticker that read "Climate Change Is Just Hot Air." I felt such a sense of envy, like when you're in third grade and there's that one kid left who still believes in Santa Claus and you wish you could be her because life was fun back then when you were little.

Manly Author was also digging in on the drought. He was out to find who controlled the water and why, what they were doing with their power, and who was profiting from all the misery.

One night we were eating dinner at a little Thai restaurant comparing notes on the glut of new fields of water-sucking almonds. Investment groups were buying land, digging wells, and planting high-dollar crops as families ran out of drinking water. The investors had the money to outlast everyone else, grabbing the fields and the water rights. Was it possible that food production could end up in the hands of a few groups that we knew little about?

I caught our reflection in the mirror. We looked grave. I once thought we would make a glamorous couple. Now we were a couple of old, worried, moth-eaten lions. I tried to feel the former longing, just for the fun of it, just for a moment, by concentrating on his well-muscled arms. But it was gone.

We had once talked about the summer we almost dated. I had told him how I'd climbed up to the balcony for the fateful call. But he didn't even remember the woman who had made potato salad. It was never really about someone else. I just wasn't his someone—or vice versa. A few months after that, he had met someone and loved her even though it didn't last long. After I came back from the Azores, I found someone I loved, even though it was a long-distance relationship. It had recently ended. It seemed fitting the break came during the drought, when everything was dying.

It had been six years since I had been to the Azores. But I started thinking of Terceira all the time. Sometimes I'd wake up at night imagining the Azorean scent of honey-sweet blossoms mixed with salty air.

I would flash on night skies so full of stars that even the recollection made me want to lean my head back and slowly revolve. I would be hiking in Sierra foothills through drought-stricken cottonwoods and think back to how my boots would sink into the dark volcanic earth of island trails cutting through a tangle of vines and subtropical trees that never lost their leaves.

Most of all, I thought of Azorean *chuva*, rain so soft, you barely noticed when it began or ended but that made you want to breathe as deeply as you could possibly breathe.

For years I kept a recording of cagarros on an ancient iPod. I still held that that sound was nature's way of guaranteeing a belly laugh. I listened to it. I needed a laugh. During this time, over and over again, I also listened to an old Bruce Cockburn song: *If this were the last night of the world, what would I do? What would I do that was different?*

One of my theories of life is called the Willy Wonka Candy Bar Theory.

The Willy Wonka Candy Bar Theory

> In British author Roald Dahl's classic *Charlie and the Chocolate Factory*, you're told that little Charlie Bucket has only one chance to find one of the golden tickets to the factory: his yearly birthday chocolate bar. He opens it and no ticket. But *then* Grandpa Joe reveals a secret silver piece, and they buy and unwrap another candy bar. No ticket. Now it's winter, and the whole family is starving because Mr. Bucket lost his job (you don't realize how grim children's books are until you're an adult), and Charlie finds a dollar. He buys a candy bar, and a ticket is the last thing on his mind because he's literally starving. He gobbles it down, not even noticing there is no ticket. Then he buys

just one more Wonka Whipple-Scrumptious Fudgemallow Delight, and there's the ticket.

The point is that you seldom ever *really* have just one shot.

In 2015, drought continued. But the earlier stories I'd written about people trying to hang on to their homes, their farms, and their dreams won the Pulitzer Prize for feature writing. I had an unexpected dollar and decided to spend it on another Willy Wonka candy bar, so to speak. I took a one-year leave from work and went back to the Azores.

If this was the last night of the world, I wanted to do something different.

A Return

The young woman who set up my Portuguese telephone number at a shop in Angra do Heroísmo, the biggest city in Terceira, looked dubious when I gave her my address.

"Serreta? But that's on the north side. I couldn't live out there," she said. "I must have stores and be able to walk to a beach."

Serreta was one of Terceira's smallest villages. I had chosen it because many had left there and not come back for decades, if at all. Serreta had "ghost houses"—unclaimed homes that sat empty for years as generations left for California, Canada, and Greater Boston. "Ruins" was a standard real estate category in the Azores. The windows of real estate offices had flyers showing crumbling stone structures. But ruins were more commonly advertised by *vende-se* spray-painted on the side of their mossy stone walls with vines sprouting out what was once a window.

It was twelve miles from Angra's cobblestone streets and outdoor cafés to Serreta. The entire potato-shaped island was about eighteen miles long and ten miles at its widest point. I rolled my eyes at my cosmopolitan phone consultant. No matter how short of space, people must always have a here and a there and a middle-of-nowhere.

There was one main road that circled the island. It was still like playing an arcade game: Don't hit the cows! Swerve around the man with the ladder in the street while he tiles his roof! But now they had added Lycra-clad speeding cyclists. Bike races and bike tours had discovered Terceira.

Other things had also changed. I rented my house from California on an app on my phone. The airline was now public and didn't allow live chickens. Still, on my way back to Serreta, there were a dozen cars backed up behind a herd of moseying cows, and that guy in the Mercedes could honk all he wanted, but cows are not easily hurried. There was still one overpass on the island, and it remained reserved for cows.

The soaring mustard-gold house on the property where I was staying had been deserted when eight heirs had emigrated, one by one. It had fallen completely to the ground in Terceira's devastating 1980 earthquake and was later restored to luxury by new owners. There were floor-to-ceiling glass doors facing the sea, two bathrooms, and a formal dining table.

This was not the house I had rented.

I was in the converted stable next door. It had been rebuilt from the original rocks. There was a bedroom built into the loft where they used to store hay. The front door was cherry red. Other than a fear of those three-foot-deep rock walls tumbling back into a heap in another earthquake, it was perfect for me and the now remarkably unflappable, if annoyingly self-determining, Murphy. He had traveled with me from California.

The loft had one window that looked out to the sea and one that framed the street leading up to the church. It was a famous church. Once, a long time ago, a miracle had taken place in Serreta. I would tell you when and what miracle, except that after a summer of asking, I never heard the same details twice. Suffice it to say that someone had once been suffering and been granted divine relief. So for the past few hundred years, every September, people who have asked God for help and received a blessing make a pilgrimage by foot around the island to Serreta, ending their journey at Igreja de Nossa Senhora dos

Milagres—Our Lady of Miracles Church. It's like the famed pilgrimage of Camino de Santiago that stretches through Portugal, France, and Spain, except it's a small island, so the walk usually takes less than four hours.

Just down from the church there was a tiny market run by Mariza, a Portuguese Canadian. Mariza had first moved to Terceira when she'd gotten engaged to an Azorean in Toronto.

"In Canada he had seemed totally normal," she said, following her first sentence by cocking one brow, pursing her lips, and nodding her head, all signs that I had better pull out the plastic crate I sat on when Mariza told a story.

"We got here, and he was close to his mother. OK, I get that. I'm very close to my family," she said, wagging a finger, spreading her hands, and clasping her chest.

"But then," she said, lifting both brows and one finger and holding them in dramatic pause, "things got a little weird."

The mother insisted on doing all her son's laundry. Once, when a pair of Mariza's underthings got mixed in, the mother announced over dinner, with tears in her eyes, that she was so glad Mariza did not wear thongs like the last girlfriend. (Mariza said she'd just happened to wear boy shorts that day.)

The mother would gaze at her son and rub his arm and say, "You will always be my man."

One day, Mariza had had enough.

"Look," she told the mother. "He is your son. He will always be your son. But he is *my* man."

The son walked in, the mother went to him, and—Mariza's outstretched arms, chopping up and down as she told this part, insisting there should be capital letters here—KISSED HIM ON THE LIPS.

"I mean really," Mariza said, sitting down. "Is it just me, or is that weird, eh?"

She had a new boyfriend now. He was good-looking and hardworking, and his mother had died young.

Mariza's mother had grown up in Serreta and was one of those who had left the Azores during the bad years. She had been so hungry as a child that she had walked down the street after the church's feast days to eat any food people had left on their plates.

Before those hard times, generations before Mariza's mother and many others had gone hungry, Serreta was a summer resort. A local historian told me it was the bathing suit that had done it in.

In the 1800s, affluent families from Angra came to cool off in summer breezes chilled by its dwarf rain forest and the spray of the waves crashing at the base of cliffs. Then European society loosened up and deemed it acceptably modest for women to wear neck-to-ankle sodden wool. Girls and women could swim! (There is nothing like visiting a place where the past hovers close to remind a woman how curtailed and oppressed her life might have been.) Soon families were building summerhouses in villages where they could actually get into the water.

Serreta isn't the place for an ocean dip. When I walked Murphy down to the lighthouse, I kept my swim-crazy Lab on a leash. One paw in those waters might mean death. Black cliffs jutted out in the ocean, their jagged edges proof of battering seas. Waves crashed into one another with cracks as elemental as thunder, throwing white froth like fireworks. The swirling pools they left behind had deadly undertows.

A beautiful lighthouse once stood near this spot. For good reason: there are more documented shipwrecks on the bottom of the ocean floor around the Azores than anywhere else in the Atlantic. But shipping routes changed, and when the lighthouse was damaged in the 1980 earthquake, they tore it down. Now there was just a squat square house with an abandoned-looking red-and-white-striped tower, but I swore I still saw a light flashing in storms.

On my walks down to the point, I often passed the same woman who always seemed to be out sweeping her front step. She would offer high-pitched sentences, and Murphy would wiggle with joy. Barbara speaks to Murphy in this exact lilt, so I knew the woman was squeaking, more or less, "Oh, aren't you pretty? Aren't you a good dog? Can you wag that tail any harder?"

There really is nothing like a dog to make the particular words unimportant. The woman and I would stand on the side of the road, beaming and nodding at each other with a mix of poorly pronounced and little-understood Portuguese and English as we both patted Murphy.

One afternoon, a man walking down the street paused and asked whether we needed a translator. Mannie, a Portuguese American with an easy affability and a summerhouse next to cornfields, had left Serreta as a ten-year-old and not returned for forty-two years. In California, he lived in Pebble Beach, and if you've ever seen that stretch of the coast, you can understand why he wasn't in too big of a hurry to roam.

Then his best friend died at fifty-one. A man who could tell a joke. A man with a roaring love of life. A man, Mannie said, who was not supposed to die at fifty-one.

Mannie went to the funeral. He didn't cry. But he felt like stone, as if his body had turned into something inanimate. He went home and told his wife, Mary, that he thought they should finally take that trip back to the Azores that they had always talked about.

After landing on Terceira, he looked around and thought, *Yeah, OK, I remember this.* He'd heard about people who broke down when they got off the plane. That wasn't him. They visited Mary's hometown, and that was nice enough.

The next day they drove to Serreta.

"We came up that big hill, and as soon as I saw the village sign, the one where you turn to go to the lighthouse, I started crying," he said. "I could feel my mother and father and my grandparents. I could even feel my great-grandparents, and I had never met them.

"I'm not that kind of guy. Not at all. But that is what happened. They were there. We went to visit the relatives, and I kept having to put on my sunglasses and look up this way and that way because for two days straight I kept breaking down."

He bought a house and fields his uncle had once owned. He and Mary and their children and grandchildren now came every year.

During one of those family vacation summers, when his two grandsons were very small, just three and five, they went missing, slipped out when no one was looking. Everyone was in a panic, searching and calling. Mannie drove down by the lighthouse. He didn't really think they could walk that far, but he'd been there with them earlier in the day picking blackberries, and he'd looked everywhere else.

They were sitting on a log, shoulder to shoulder, facing the sea.

Mannie walked over.

"So, hey there, what are you doing?" he asked.

"Looking," they both said.

Mannie said it was one of his proudest moments.

"They were just sitting there, really looking at the ocean. At my island," he said.

The Marching Band of Livingston

It was an unusually gray May and early June. The air was damp and cool. At Abismo, the snack bar near the Biscoitos lava pools where I used to eat ice cream with John, a woman wrinkled her nose at her pasty child.

"Usually by now, he's such a pretty color," she told her visiting relatives.

"And I'm wearing a sweater," she said sadly, plucking at the offending knit.

Worry was growing that the weather would not be good for Sanjoaninas, the weeklong festa that kicks off the festa season.

One morning, I woke up even earlier than the daily bread delivery, which I was delighted to find was still part of daily life. I walked over and looked out the window at the sea as always but this time jumped back. There were two islands that hadn't been out there before.

The islands of São Jorge and Graciosa seemed as close as bobbing toys in a bathtub. It was no wonder that it took hundreds of years to get all nine Azorean Islands charted, if they kept appearing and disappearing like this.

The sea was deep-blue enamel, edged in purple. Leaden skies had given way to puffy white clouds stamped on pretty, pastel blue.

It was the same morning as the arrival of one of the season's first "summer planes"—direct flights from the United States and Canada timed to the festas. I didn't know anyone coming in, but their arrival seemed as good a reason as any to take a drive around the island.

After getting off a plane at the Lajes airport, a man dropped to all fours and kissed the tarmac.

He wasn't a nervous flyer; Norbeto took just one whiff of Azorean air—the scent of laurel and grass and ocean, nine hundred miles from the pollution of population centers—and down he went. He hadn't been back in more than forty years.

No one was more surprised by this show of emotion than Norbeto's son Nelson, who had been trying unsuccessfully for years to get his father to visit: "I'd tell him, 'Dad, we're taking the kids back—your grandchildren. Come with us. I'll buy you a ticket.' He always said no."

Norbeto said what he remembered most about the Azores was how hard he'd worked to start a new life away from there.

"When I got to California, I worked in a lot of cow shit and I didn't sleep too much, and after three days I looked at my check, and it was nothing," he said. "But in the Azores, there was no shoes, no electricity, no food. There was too much crying. I was scared to go back and remember the crying."

Norbeto had finally come back because his grandkids' band was going to march down Angra's Main Street.

Two years earlier the Filarmônica Lira Açoriana de Livingston—the Azorean Marching Band of Livingston—received an invitation to be part of Sanjoaninas. Livingston is a small town in a part of California where a dairy is about as likely to be owned by an Azorean as it is to have cows.

The group hosted pork dinners and auctioned livestock and sold homemade Portuguese pastries to raise money. They added new songs and doubled up on rehearsals.

As excitement grew about their trip to the Azores, grandparents, godparents, aunts, uncles, parents, and pals started thinking maybe this would be a good time for them to go back too. Including Norbeto, who had once played clarinet in his hometown in the Azores but didn't have time for such things in California. The band had about fifty members, but the group that arrived in Terceira, many of them on Norbeto's flight, was close to three hundred people.

I saw Norbeto and Nelson a few days later at an afternoon party. Nelson looked tired.

"My dad is out of control," he said. "It's like being the father of a bad teenager."

His seventy-year-old father would leave the house in the morning, expected home for lunch. He'd come back late, near dawn the next day, telling of running into this friend and that friend and losing track of time at a party.

"And I'm saying, 'But couldn't you have at least called so we wouldn't worry?'" Nelson said.

On the other side of the island, Angra do Heroísmo was a tangle of festa preparation. Narrow cobblestone streets were closed. There were so many detour signs busy pointing, they appeared to contradict one another. There was the *beep-beep* of trucks backing up and the *ping-ping* of hammering. Men in safety vests scrambled up poles like colonies of fluorescent ants.

Finally, opening night arrived. Arches of white lights were strung down the main avenues, between stately seventeenth- and eighteenth-century buildings. Within each arch hung a colorful lit-up beer stein. (OK, it was really the city's coat of arms. I'm nearsighted.) Red carpets rolled across streets, accenting the distinctive Portuguese patterns made from black basalt and white limestone. Colorful, intricate quilts made especially for the festa, some of which had been passed down for generations, draped from balconies and second-story windows.

Crowds lined the street ten people deep.

I was fortunate to be invited to a party at a house on Angra's most venerable avenue. I had an enviable view from the balcony, as well as a peek at life with heirloom rugs and works of art and dark, antique wood furniture and walls of books. The guests were professors and doctors and such whose families had quite literally known one another for centuries. It was like having good seats at a concert when you really want to be down on the floor dancing near the stage.

Each year a beautiful girl is chosen to be the queen of the festa. My hostess, Ana Barbara, a beautiful woman in her forties, had been a queen when she was seventeen. Instead of the usual glitzy ball gown, they dressed her as Queen Dona Amélia in a sober gown, understated makeup, and pulled-back hair.

Dona Amélia was the last queen of Portugal. She sang and painted and went to medical school mostly to care for her husband, King Carlos, as he aged. She and her son Manuel, who would become the last king of Portugal, survived an assassination attack that killed her husband and her other son, Prince Luis Felipe.

Ana Barbara remembers people crying when they saw her—not just the usual queen but Queen Amélia, a symbol of resilience.

I knew the name because of pastries. In the oldest part of Angra, there is the bakery O Forno. They are famous for their *Bolos D. Amélias*, namesake little cakes that are a Terceiran specialty. The story of the cakes is on each elegant white box including an English translation:

> First of all there was good land. Then the people came and started sowing cereals. Later on they brought the precious spices of exotic tastes and strange scents from East and

> West Indias. In a typically Portuguese way, they mixed it all with magic and wise hands. They made new and delicious recipes.
>
> When D. Amélia, the last Portuguese Queen, visited the island for the first time, the inhabitants made very special cakes that took her name.

The cakes were little and round, dark and sweet and spicy and very soft—right on the edge of pudding—with a generous dusting of powdered sugar. I ate far too many of them.

Ana Barbara approached and drew me inside.

"There's someone you should meet," she said. "He's a man of influence in California."

The man turned around as we drew near, and he and I both said, "You! I know you!"

This was no stuffed shirt—this was Manuel Vieira, the Sweet Potato King.

During Vieira's reign, the sweet potato had changed from something people mostly bought at Thanksgiving to fries and chips and body butter, and no doubt they will next be fueling jet packs or fixing under-eye bags. The Central Valley produces about 90 percent of California's sweet potatoes. As a reporter, I'd often crossed paths with Vieira.

At our first meeting I'd asked him who exactly had christened him the Sweet Potato King.

"I did!" he'd said with enthusiasm. "I even paid a guy to write a book!"

Once at a cattle auction in California, I bumped into a bunch of kids at a table singing in Portuguese. They were a marching band from Manuel's little hometown on the island of Pico. He paid their way over for a California festa and then decided to send everyone to Disneyland and for a day in San Francisco as well. Now he'd chipped in to bring a small-town California band to the Azores during a drought when many farm families couldn't afford full-price fare.

We moved to the balcony to watch the parade of dance troupes and floats representing the curves and swirls of ocean waves, fantastical sea dragons, and sailing ships. The Livingston band was getting closer. They were resplendent in their gold-buttoned burgundy jackets, white pants, white shoes, and gold-braided caps. No production of *The Music Man* was ever more diligently costumed.

Manuel was beaming and pounding my back in glee.

"Diana, I feel the tears begin to form," he said as big fat drops slid down his face, despite a big fat grin. "Come," he said. "Let's get down there."

We ran down the stairs and out the door and pushed our way into the street with the marching band. Once we were trotting along with the musicians, it was somehow quieter. We weaved through the drummers, nodding apologies to the flutists and clarinetists and tubaists, until Manuel could hop backward alongside his trumpeter grandson shouting, "Here, here, take a picture." We didn't catch up to the grandson playing trombone until the city's square, where the parade ended.

A float carrying three young women in sparkly gowns pulled up for them to disembark. They wore sashes declaring them to be Miss Gustine, California; Miss Canada; and Miss Eastern United States. As Miss Eastern US descended a wobbly rolling staircase, a woman shouted, "Everybody's looking at you! Everybody's looking at you!" I thought she meant the crowd but then saw a woman holding up a tablet. The girl's grandmother and aunts were crammed together on a sofa in East Providence, Rhode Island.

"They're saying, 'We love you!'" the woman screamed, knocking on the screen.

When Miss Gustine came down the stairs, a man shouted, "Viva California!" and the crowd took up the chant: "Viva California! Viva California!"

I asked people around me about their connection to California, something that would become a habit all summer.

"Two aunts in Chowchilla."

"My brother lives in Gustine."

"I worked on a dairy in Hanford. Too much work."

The man who started the California chant was Boston real estate agent Victor Santos. "On Monday, it will be forty-six years since I left this place," he said. "But I always keep it with me."

The year before, his older daughter had been Miss Eastern US, and he'd been proud that she was representing Azorean emigrants. But standing beside him on this night was his younger daughter, twenty-one-year-old Chelsie, who was taking it further. She wanted to move to the Azores for good. She thought she might have a job lined up at a friend's beauty shop.

"It's too far away!" her father exclaimed.

Chelsie said it was too complicated in the United States, always shifting between American and Azorean identity. She said when she was on the island, she could just be herself. It felt as if she was home, she said.

Home—it seemed like a fragile idea to me. Is it where we're from or where we are?

There was a reception for the Livingston band in the city hall, the neoclassical building that anchored the square. Inside, red carpet rolled down a marble staircase. The mayor of Angra had offered me a tour of the building, and I noticed he walked off to the side of the carpet.

"I've learned those red carpets can slide—safer over here," he said, which I took to be life advice.

The Sweet Potato King joined us.

"I just can't get over it: thirty-two years ago we start a little band, and we're here tonight," he said, trying not to cry again but not succeeding.

"People are going to be talking about this for a very long time," said the mayor.

I wandered outside. Through the crowd I noticed this year's festa court posing for photos. There was something familiar about the teenage boy who was the festa king. I couldn't get any closer because the square was crowded with revelers. I watched for a long time. But I couldn't place him.

A Reference Point

One of the first people I got in contact with in Terceira (besides Chef, who picked Murphy and me up at the airport, late and smoking a cigarette, so at least I knew that there would be some things the same) was Luís, whom I'd met in California just before my trip. I had gone to a gig Luís was playing at the Lucky Strike Lanes on Sunset Boulevard in Hollywood. He was backing up his daughter Maria's rock act, but Luís was the reason the audience was peppered with LA's best guitar players. He was world-class and well known in their circles.

While the rest of the band took a break, Luís played a solo. Alone onstage in a Portuguese white shirt with flowing sleeves, he sat on a stool. He held the guitar facing him and curved his body toward it, enclosing the space between.

He played a melody with pauses and echoes of traditional Azorean songs that grew into a rhythm that had the whole crowd pulsating, rocking back and forth, driving with him.

The audience was young, mostly from Artesia, the pocket of Azores re-created near Los Angeles. They went wild. The man next to me, who said he worked as a studio musician, slapped his leg.

"And that, ladies and gentleman, is what you call genius," he said to no one in particular.

I had emailed Luís earlier, arranging to meet him. After the concert, sweaty and breathing hard, he tried to make his way to me at the bar. He was repeatedly stalled by groups of admirers. He was sixty but looked younger, despite a rock 'n' roll youth of late gigs and excesses in Boston. He had dark eyes that dipped at the corners, adding a melancholy touch to his face. We had to wait until the bartender was emptying glasses and the crowd dwindled before we could hear each other.

His was the Azorean migration tale in reverse: he went back to stay, and he went to the States to visit family. When he was a twenty-nine-year-old immigrant in Boston, he felt he wasn't whole. He had to tamp down the Azorean part of him that instinctively kissed everyone on the cheek—men and women. The side of him that was quick to hug and cry. He didn't voice his passionate opinions about America's inequalities because, in his working-class neighborhood, they would have told him to go back where he came from. Even though he'd come at fifteen.

He learned to fit into a world that said he shouldn't still live with his mother and brothers after eighteen, shouldn't stop his car in the middle of the street to chat with a neighbor. Even love—he wasn't supposed to get too carried away and speak all the words in his heart, or the object of his passion would think he was crazy. That kept happening.

For years he had a driving hunger to make it on the music scene. Before he was thirty, he had one of the hottest bands in Boston. His little brother Nuno, whom he'd taught guitar, found fame with the 1990s band Extreme.

But Luís still didn't feel centered.

"I got so good at flipping back and forth between ways of seeing the world, ways of being in the world, that I didn't know what inside me was authentic," he recalled.

He decided he needed a quick vacation. He grabbed a cheap airfare from Boston to São Miguel Island. It was supposed to be a three-day trip to soak in some sun, visit a few old friends, and maybe set up a band tour.

He had no plans of going to Terceira, the island where he'd grown up. But at the airport, when it was time to go back to the Unites States, he hid from his flight. He let them keep calling his name, and he didn't know why. He bought a ticket to Terceira—a thirty-minute trip. He went to the house where he'd grown up. He asked the people who lived in the house whether he could come inside.

From a second-story window he watched an older woman walking to Mass. She was an old friend of the family's. She walked slowly, pausing every few yards to catch her breath. When she paused, she would look around, scanning the houses, gazing out at the sea. She would lift her face to the breeze. Every time she paused, he would remember loud, nasal voices of family and friends gathered in the kitchen together, swimming in the ocean, and what he felt like to have one self.

"I didn't have a reference point, nothing that held steady," he told me. "I decided it would be her. I would move back, and every day I would watch this woman walk to Mass because that was real."

He was not a religious man—Luís even liked to shock people a little by announcing he hated God. But for decades, until she died, he watched an old woman walk to daily Mass. He still pauses every afternoon to picture that walk. He says it is his one steady thing.

On Terceira, Luís and the friend he was introducing were waiting for me at a little café in Praia. The man worked for the Azorean government and was negotiating with the Chinese to lease parts of Lajes Air Force Base that the Americans were deserting.

The American base had been a part of Terceira's culture since World War II. My favorite summary of its significance came from a creatively translated guidebook they once gave away free at local hotels:

> The base brought to the island a little of the "American Way of Living." To a great number of inhabitants, it gave access to American clubs and mess, allowing the intercourse—and the purchase of many goods that would only appear much later on other markets at unreasonable prices.
>
> —*Book of Terceira Island*

The Americans had now largely pulled out of Lajes Air Force Base, taking their mess and intercourse and goods for purchase and devastating the island's economy. The people who had rented houses to military families or run nearby restaurants or sold supplies had lost income at the height of the European Debt Crisis, a contagion that started in the United States with the subprime mortgage crisis.

Actually, the US military has not taken their mess with them. The Azorean regional government was pressing the United States to pay for environmental cleanup from seventy years of a military base. The United States was balking.

I had some questions about what needed to be cleaned up.

On my first trip I heard stories about convoys that drove into the interior of the island. The Portuguese workers would be told to wait with the trucks. The American soldiers would carry something from the trucks and come back much later without it.

"Did they bury bombs in Terceira? Or are these just bar stories?" I asked Luís's friend. "Are there documents?"

"I don't know. I wouldn't be surprised. That's how they used to dispose of old weapons," he said. "I thought you were interested in the site where there was nuclear testing."

He said there was a hill on the base where nothing—"and I mean nothing"—has grown for more than fifty years. Not a single blade of grass. Old photos showed it lush like the rest of the island.

I felt a chill. I know that sounds like a cliché. But something inside me shivered.

When we were leaving, my eyes focused on a photo hanging on the wall of the busy café. I grabbed Luís's arm.

"*What* is that? *Why* do they have a framed picture of Salazar?" I said, more loudly than polite conversation would call for. I wanted the owners to hear me questioning why they had a fascist dictator on their wall.

Luís wrinkled his nose. "Eh, it's people being people," he said. "Times are tough. They're losing money. They say Salazar was good for business."

I drove out of my way to stop at the fire station on the way home. Chef was there, which was usual now. The crisis had wiped out many social services, so emergency workers had far greater workloads, and he was working double shifts. Firefighters were sometimes the only option for an elderly person who had fallen out of bed.

I told him about the Salazar photo.

His jaw set in a way I had never seen before, as if his face were carved in stone.

"There are dark things loose in this world right now," he said.

Even here, I thought. *Even on this beautiful island.*

There was a time Chef would never have gone more than a day without jumping into the ocean or playing music with his friends. Now he worked all the time. What choice did he have? He'd completed his degree. But he wasn't ready yet to work in an office.

"I need to go diving," he said. "I get cranky when I'm too long from the water."

I flashed on a quote attributed to Gandhi that Moody used to keep pinned up in the photographers' cubicle at work: "Almost anything you do will be insignificant, but you must do it . . . We do these things not to change the world, but so that the world will not change us."

I was just beginning to understand how hard a task this is.

The Cão Who Ate the Pão

One morning early in the summer, before neighborly forbearance could be curried, Murphy took off. He did this in the manner that annoys me the most: pausing when I called his name, one paw crooked delicately in the air, a moment of eye contact letting me know he considered my plea before carrying on his merry way, unheeded.

Murphy has many redeeming qualities.

By this you will immediately understand that he does not always come when called, chases cows and cats (although if the poor hassled feline stops, he sits dumbfounded and merely projects a friendly curiosity), and eats everything.

Life with Murphy is like sharing quarters with a marauding bear. After he learned how to open two different bread boxes, I briefly thought about getting a Yosemite bear canister, but I lack the counter space.

Before judging him too harshly, one must consider that Murphy has a defective gene. A team of scientists in the United Kingdom, Sweden, and the United States researching Lab gluttony found that many of his kind have a scrambled version of POMC (proopiomelanocortin), the gene that helps regulate appetite. "Labradors are not only the most commonly overweight breed of dog, but they are notorious for being obsessed by food," lead researcher Eleanor Raffan told a reporter in 2016. "Some particularly badly [obsessed] dogs will eat things no other creature would want to consume."

Until this particular day, the most notorious items on the What Murphy Ate list had included a *rosca de reis* (three kings' cake) large enough for fifteen servings and its plastic baby Jesus, which according to Mexican tradition meant he was blessed and should host a tamale party (how he got said cake off the *top* of the refrigerator remains a mystery), a pair of raw-linen Sur La Table dinner napkins (wiped with hands that had touched food), and an entire raw onion.

Britain's fattest pet, a 176-pound Labrador named Alfie, described by one official as "a massive blob with a leg at each corner," was referenced in the *New York Times* story about the gluttonous Lab research.

Murphy at least is not fat (thus far), but that just leaves him spry enough to sprint about forever in search of food.

I followed him up the steep *canada*—avenue—that the cows came down every morning. I hoped they were off nibbling a green Azorean hillside, lessening the chance Murphy would get himself kicked in the head.

I briefly considered humanity's relationship to beauty in our environment.

I had often driven down Blackstone Avenue in Fresno, its gray asphalt the same color as the smoggy sky. There was a jangly lineup of businesses offering smog tests, reptiles, oil changes, sex toys, waffles, Chinese food buffets, and midnight tacos.

I was a reporter, so the landscape was dotted with anecdotes: "Oh, that's the corner where the cops fired so many bullets, they ran out of evidence markers the next day and they didn't hit the guy they were aiming for, but the girlfriend." Across the street was the tire store where an angry prostitute had accused me of encroaching on her territory when I was doing interviews about another shooting. ("I am wearing a khaki skirt and scuffed ballet flats," I told her wearily. "Nothing more clearly states reporter, not hooker.")

I had wondered on more than one occasion whether simply driving down Blackstone sucked my soul. So did it then follow that walking a lane in sight of a long stretch of sea elevated the human spirit?

The climb was steep, and in no time I looked over green pastures divided by volcanic rock walls and, beyond that, the sea. It was a day of powder blues and soft grays. Stripes of clouds on the horizon made it impossible to tell exactly where sky and ocean met.

My reveries about the benefits of beauty were interrupted when I saw Murphy up ahead with a plastic bag.

One of the plastic bags the bread man left on the doors in the morning.

Quickly, I looked up and down the street and felt relief to see bags still hanging on doors. Until I realized the bottoms of all the bags were gone, as were the fresh-baked *paposeco*—rolls with crispy crusts—that they had held. Murphy had eaten my entire neighborhood's breakfasts.

My heart began beating faster, dismay spreading from my head to my feet. To understand my panic, you must understand the Portuguese fealty to fresh bread. It is *religious*, right up there with church and soccer.

One day I asked my neighbor, a professor with a kind but formal air, how I, too, could get bread delivery. He told me I needed only to wave down the bread van and put in an order. The next morning I found the professor standing in the rain, holding an umbrella, in the middle of the street.

"I am sorry, Diana, but may I have a word?" he asked. "I am waiting to speak to the bread man because he may not—pardon—understand your Portuguese."

I was pleased to find that the professor considered me to have any Portuguese, however unintelligible.

"But perhaps this is not the bread man you want?" he asked. "This bakery delivers at seven thirty in the morning. Perhaps you prefer to sleep in? There is another bakery that delivers at eight thirty, but they do not deliver on Sunday. This bakery delivers on Sunday. But not at seven thirty, at ten thirty."

I do prefer to sleep in. But when a neighbor is standing in the rain for you, it is best to agree to Bakery Number One.

The point of this story is that in a place where a village of three hundred supports two rival bread delivery services and a place where you wouldn't want to eat seven-thirty bread at eight thirty, my dog had eaten everyone's favorite morning carbohydrates.

The night before the bread incident, I had gone to a book launch party for Joel Neto, an Azorean writer. We had exchanged numbers to meet later and discuss Azorean identity and writer's neuroses. But now I called Joel for one reason only: he had a *cão*—a dog.

"Oh, this is bad," Joel said when I explained the situation. "The *pão*"—bread—"is very important in the Azores."

At least there wasn't blood involved. Joel told me their dog Melville had once eaten two of his neighbor's chickens.

"It was horrible. They were very nice chickens. My neighbors were very fond of their chickens," he said. "The rooster had a Facebook page."

Joel had given them four new chickens and suggested a similar plan for me. He told me to go immediately to a good bakery and get replacement bread and also bonus cookies. He texted me a message in Portuguese to copy and include with my offerings.

There were few people stirring (or they had already gone off for the day unfed) as I dropped off my half-dozen bags of bread, cookies, and a witty note that summed up to "I'm sorry my dog, Murphy, ate your bread," authored by a guy whose books were in the window of bookstores all over Portugal.

More troublesome than my gluttonous dog was my *sucata*—piece of junk—car. I had bought it sight unseen while I was still in California. I knew the Azorean code that you took care of those in the circle. It was the same way that in Fresno, if I needed new tires or a phone or insurance, I would call Patrick, Armen and Odie's son. He always "had a guy"—a fellow Armenian. I had no definitive ethnicity of my own but relied on others with tribe members.

Elmano, my Azorean professor friend in California, had sent out an email on my behalf, and the man married to Elmano's cousin's wife's sister said he had a dependable transportation car for 1,500 euros.

Sold.

The man married to Elmano's cousin's wife's sister delivered the car, and I gave him a ride home. There he threw in a bottle of wine and a big cabbage from his garden. He said we'd do the paperwork and I'd give him the money when Elmano arrived for his summer stay.

The car was huge by Azorean standards—an old American Honda with automatic transmission that was roughly twice as wide as a European street car and just about as wide as many island roads.

It was purple. Some will contradict me on this. Elmano, when he arrived, thought it looked black. Many hold with blue. But I say definitively purple. It mostly depended on how the sun hit its metallic-flake paint job. I named the car Barney, after the children's-show dinosaur: big, purple, and obnoxious.

As I was driving home, it started to rain, which happened often but was still not something I took for granted after watching California shrivel. The front windshield leaked a little, which they had warned Elmano about. But soon water was leaking freely from the roof like fake rain in a Las Vegas rain forest. I had water running down my face. The windshield wipers didn't turn on. One headlight didn't either. The engine was making an ominous *va-va-va-ROOM-ROOM*. The accented syllable was all wrong.

Still, I was ecstatic. Look at me: Not just a tourist. I owned an automobile.

I stopped at the fire station in my old village to show Chef my new car.

He took a long look at Barney, stood back, and nodded.

"Oh, I see," he said. "You have bought a car for life. Because no one else will ever buy this car."

He looked even more tired. Public servants in a crashing economy were spread thin. The days when we could spend leisurely afternoons at the fire station were gone.

On the days Barney would start, I'd tell Murphy, "Load up," and drive down the hill through Serreta's forest of laurel trees and around a wide swoop of curve that overlooked cornfields and open sea, passing the four-hundred-year-old villages of houses with red-tile roofs and always a church, a café, and a bar in the center of town. Murphy was a backseat driver, keeping his nose next to my ear and snorting at every turn until we reached the Biscoitos pools.

Everyone from lithesome teens to luxuriously fat grandparents sunbathed on the concrete platforms like seals piled on rocks. I bypassed the crowds and went to an isolated cove where Murphy could swim without disturbing anyone, other than the gulls that dive-bombed him for being too close to their nests.

After Murphy's swim, I would, as the Portuguese phrased it, "take a coffee," sitting at one of the bright-orange plastic tables at the Abismo snack bar while Murphy napped at my feet on the cobblestone patio.

One day, a young man approached to pet him. Murphy wiggled groggily to his feet (calm friendliness being one of his aforementioned traits of redemption).

"He is a Labrador retriever?" the man asked in English. "What's his name?"

I said Murphy.

"Murphy the Labrador?!" he asked. "Why, this is the *Cão* Who Ate the *Pão*!"

Moody

I was sitting in the spot above Murphy's lava-rock pool where I sat most days, marveling at the water's changing colors. It could be the deepest blue or lavender or frothing aqua. Even the rocks changed from algae green to chalky gray to shiny black depending on the tides.

The one constant was Murphy's high-pitched yelping while he swam in circles and splashed and dipped his head beneath water. He was an odd-duck dog. I was strategically positioned at the top of the footpath to the pools, so I could grab him if he got out of the water and made a run to the dumpster in the parking lot.

My phone rang. It was Jack Moody.

It was fitting that he should call when I was gazing across the ocean because that's when I thought of home. I could feel it there across the water. Well, across the water and about three thousand miles of land. I was looking at the Atlantic. California faces a different ocean.

I figured it would be a short conversation because Moody doesn't like talking on the phone. It was traits like this that made me consider him cranky. In turn, he sometimes called me perky or chipper, which offended me deeply.

There is a piece of backstory here that I have left out. I'm sorry to have buried it in this telling. But it was something never spoken of, even by us. It was buried in real life as well. It happened even after I found out Moody was someone with black mold in his water bottles, when I was heartbroken over someone else. Let's call it the Verbose Story.

The Verbose Story

Some things are destined. This was not one of them. I fully believe if we had just gone to our usual joint for fish tacos and beer, like usual, nothing would have happened. But it was my turn to buy, and anyway a freelance check had left me feeling expansive, so I told Moody, "Let's walk to the Italian place for gnocchi and nice wine."

It's expensive, but Louie the Lip owns the place, and every once in a while, you have to frequent a neighborhood establishment owned by a guy who goes by Louie the Lip and can tell you stories about how he got that nickname.

I didn't know it yet, but it was the day Moody had decided to take early retirement. His dream as a young traveler had been to be a world-trotting photographer. But when he married and had two children, he settled into a staff photographer position at a medium-sized paper that let him get home on time most nights so he could make being a father his main job. The marriage ended before I met him (although in our gossip-wired neighborhood, I'd heard all about his ex-wife and the tai chi instructor). I watched his two kids grow up down the street. They'd moved out on their own the previous summer. Moody was going to sell his house and literally go fishing, for months, maybe years, he said. He was determined to never photograph community theater or a sports game again.

When we got back to my place and settled in to sober up, a wine-soaked melancholy took hold of me. Everything kept changing in our neighborhood, people moving, people dying. I even felt sad about the tree on the corner the new neighbors cut down. And now Moody would be gone too. I put my head on his shoulder. There had never been an attraction between us, despite all the snark I got from women interested in him, so this should not have been a big deal. But from the millisecond we touched, we froze, like dogs on point. Perfectly still but hyperaware.

We started kissing and kept kissing, like two aged teenagers making out on a couch. I knew one of us was going to call a halt to this nonsense at any moment.

It was Moody who pulled back suddenly, I thought to put a stop to things.

"Shall we move this into the bedroom?" he asked. "Murphy keeps licking my other ear."

With each slow step across the living room, I thought in a chant, *This is a mistake, turn around. This is a mistake, turn around.* But I didn't.

You know those movies where there is an unexpected coupling and they wake with shock and horror when they realize what they've done? The camera freezing on their wild eyes as if they've learned they murdered someone while sleepwalking? I once found that ludicrous.

It's exactly right. The next morning, among other things, I was panicked I'd lost my most readily available dogsitter. It's easier to impose on platonic friends. Moody looked at me as though I'd thrown out all his favorite fishing flies.

We avoided each other for weeks. No small feat in a neighborhood where everyone walks to the same everything: market, bar, sushi place, dry cleaner, bike repair shop.

But then I started thinking (always the first sign of trouble) about how Moody let me read him pieces of my unfinished novels and he fixed my gate and we played Ping-Pong, and well, I wondered, would it be nice to be with someone who was part of my life instead of someone who was so dashing, he had no time to call among all the derring-do?

I became convinced. Why, this was a classic romantic story line: The man who was right under my nose the whole time! The one I had never suspected!

I ran down to his house like some dewy-eyed ingénue, having forgotten that I was not.

"You know that night I put my head on your shoulder?" I started in as soon as he opened the door. "It felt nice."

He was nodding yes.

"And life is so short and every moment counts and a person shouldn't just pine away for someone not there, especially if that person can't even pick up the phone, and I think we should date," I said.

He blanched.

"I thought you were doing the 'that was really nice, but' thing," he sputtered.

He wanted to know, how could we just go from the way we always were to something we were not? And he didn't want to start something where he was just waiting for it to end. And also he really liked living alone. (Note: I had said that I thought it might be nice to date. I at no point suggested moving in.)

He told me that he'd told his brother what had happened, and his brother thought it was great because his *brother* had always thought I was attractive. He seemed puzzled that someone thought this.

It was a bad idea, he said. He just wasn't verbose like me.

Verbose.

I offered to date him, and he called me verbose.

Which was why I was now pretty speechless, sitting in the Azores, when he said he was calling to tell me that he wasn't going to let what we had slip away.

The month before I left, we had fallen into a routine of taking Murphy to the park and throwing the ball and making dinner and sometimes spending nights together. Ever since he stopped working, Moody had been far less moody. He roughhoused with Murphy and danced me around the kitchen when one of those old crooner songs he liked came on the college radio station. We had gone in on one of those meal-kit services and made things like *shakshuka* and Ethiopian-spiced chicken thighs from premeasured ingredients. It was an idea based in practicality, especially for him, since he'd already packed up his kitchen. It was more fun than I had expected because the different cuisines got Moody talking about his different travels. The man was getting downright chatty.

But I thought the comfort level was because he was moving north and I was leaving for the middle of the Atlantic. We were as good as gone in different directions—simply finding each other a comfort in a time of goodbyes.

No way was I going to think it was more.

For one thing, I didn't want more. I felt I was done with all of that. Not in a bitter "I'll never fall in love again" way. But I had loved the dashing-one-from-afar, and in almost every memory we were laughing. Mary had been right: love exists, it's powerful, it's a real crack-up. Before

I had always been searching, afraid that I would never experience that. Now I'd had my turn. I figured it was like a baseball player retiring after an excellent season, topping off a long career. Best just left there. Even though, obviously, I wasn't quite ready for the nunnery.

Also, I remembered very vividly what had happened before when I thought there might be something between Moody and me.

"But you have never even liked me," I told him now.

"What are you talking about? I always liked you. I thought you were weird, but I liked you," he said. "I was just never attracted to you *at all.*"

I said the emphasized "at all" was not really necessary. He said it wasn't the way he felt now.

He said he hadn't realized how bitter he'd let himself get. He felt he was finally back to who he really was, and he wanted to be happy and that had a lot to do with me and my optimism. (I thought that sounded perilously close to perky.)

"It can take a really long time for someone to get over something," he said. "I failed at something important."

I suddenly felt sad that all those years I thought Jack was moody, he was really just broken and I hadn't been kind enough to see it.

But I wasn't buying this sudden declaration.

"I think it's strange none of this occurred to you when I was there. This keeps happening to me: I am loved . . . from afar."

"I'll come there," he said. "Tell me when."

"What do you want?" I asked suspiciously.

Moody laughed.

"I'm not sure," he said. "But nothing is off the table. I've been an inconsistent lover, even friend. You have every reason to question this. But what I am telling you is that I want this to last. I want to try. And I haven't said that to anyone in fifteen years."

My eyes were watering, and I didn't know why. As far as I knew, I hadn't been pining for Jack Moody.

"What about before?" I asked. "You called me verbose."

"Well . . . ," Moody said, trailing off, indicating he certainly didn't find me mute. "But also that may have been the most terrified I've been in my life. I needed to think."

(For years.)

"Don't answer now," he said. "Think about it." He said he could come anytime between his annual summer fishing trip with the guys and hunting pheasant with his brother in late fall. Oh, how I hated his yearly donning of camouflage and trying to get me to eat game.

"I know you're thinking you could never date someone who hunts," he said. "So, Marcum, I promise you that I'm a terrible shot. It's a brother bonding thing. The birds are safe."

Lost Summer Love

In the Azores' long history of exodus, the most common reason for a stay or a go, a hold steady or a leap, was love. (Although I suppose that's true everywhere.)

Chef even told me about a family that had changed countries every generation. The great-grandmother married an Azorean American and moved to California. They brought their daughter back for the summer, and she fell in love with an Azorean and stayed. Her son married an Azorean Canadian he'd met during her family's summer vacation and immigrated to Toronto. Now that couple's daughter was marrying an Azorean from California, and they were starting a business in Terceira.

I started crowdsourcing love stories during a lunch with Luís, the guitar artist.

"Forget about it," he told me. "Summer love isn't part of this place anymore."

"What are you talking about?" I asked.

"This new generation doesn't fall in love. They don't even know how to have a summer flirt," he said. "There are no goodbyes, only catch-you-laters. There is no excitement of the other. It's all global now. Same haircut. Same music. Most of all, there's no inner self. What's there to allow someone to discover? They put it on Facebook."

Earlier, during the soup course, Luís had spoken fervently of the reason for music and pondered, What is truth? What is happiness? Must sorrow be part of life? (Absolutely, held Luís.)

I had wanted to ask what kind of soup we were eating but never got a chance.

I said to him, "Luís, I do believe you love the intangible."

"Ah. No, you don't understand me at all," Luís said with the rueful laugh of one sadly used to being misunderstood. "And. Anyway," he said, leaning forward, cupping his chin on his hand, narrowing his eyes, "what *is* intangible? Really?"

He let the question linger. Then nodded at having, apparently, made his point.

In California, he had told me it might prove inconvenient for me to be seen with him, as he was the most hated man on the island. Then when I arrived, he introduced me to his sprawling network of dear friends. But I understood how he might rub some people the wrong way.

One night he was playing on São Miguel, the most populated island. A table of people from Terceira were loudly and drunkenly cheering him on.

"We love you, Luís. We are your fans. We, too, are from Terceira."

From the stage, Luís told them he had never seen them at any of his concerts in Terceira. Not once. So don't pretend to be his fans on São Miguel.

"I just hate hypocrites," he said before going back to playing.

There was a payoff to Luís's madness, if it was madness. He was an artist, an astonishing and unique guitar player.

I reminded him now of how the mostly Azorean audience in Hollywood had responded to his music. "C'mon, Luís, if these kids have no passion, what are they responding to when you play guitar?"

Luís sniffed his disdain. He said he thought it was like amputees who get ghost pains in limbs no longer there. A ghostly surge of excitement in anemic hearts.

I was amused at Luís's declaration of the end of love and recounted it to Chef, thinking it was a funny story.

"No, he's right," he said. "Everyone's noticed. It's been three or four years now. Love stories don't happen here anymore. Do you remember Jaime?" he asked.

I did. He was the best diver at Belo Abismo, leaping from the highest points, flipping and turning as if he had been given immunity from gravity. Even walking down the street, he jumped up on rock walls and leaped across their gaps. He was young and suntanned, taut and muscular. His dream was to leave the island and become an international sensation in parkour, the art of maneuvering through, on, and over obstacles.

"Well, Mrs. Cardoso's granddaughter was here last summer," Chef said. "She is a beautiful girl. She saw Jaime. He saw her. OK, so people are all ready to notice them walking down the street or kissing in doorways and have something to gossip about. And what happened was Jamie was always checking his phone to see whether she had texted him.

"Azorean nights! Stars! This girl is down the street, and he is looking at his phone! We romantics are the old guard now. Love, even sex, is for dinosaurs."

I rolled my eyes. "Funny how you think the newspapers would have at least run an obituary," I said.

I was again getting much of my news through emails from Barbara, who sent links and added her own commentary. Wi-Fi was everywhere now, I could easily read a newspaper on my phone, but I just liked Barbara's curation. Shortly after this, she sent an article about how millennials were having less sex than previous generations.

The various theories included it being an unusually cautious generation because they had grown up with the likes of bicycle helmets, that they were too busy trying to make money in economically grim times, and that they hadn't learned how to spend time alone together without the distraction of electronic devices. "They're more interested in Pokémon!" she wrote in disgust.

The next day, I saw teenagers near the famous Serreta church chasing phone-generated Pokémon phantoms. Luckily it was a one-day fad.

To be clear-eyed about it, not all the islands' old summer loves had been about unbridled passion. There was a pragmatic side. For many years, one of the few ways to leave the Azores was to marry and get a green card. I remembered Romana telling me that if a girl had an American passport, she was pretty and she could sing too. And all American men were six foot two no matter what the tape measure said. But mixing love and motives—or suspicions about motives—can cause misunderstandings that haunt a half century later.

One afternoon, Elmano and Albertina, who had arrived for their summer stay, invited me to lunch to meet their friend Maria Elvita. It was her first trip back to the Azores in fifty years. It was hard to believe she was sixty-seven. She had smooth skin, lively eyes, and a sense of style, wearing a long, summery cardigan. It made it easy to picture her as a seventeen-year-old on her father's porch as she began to tell us a story from back then.

She had first seen her love at a *tourada à corda*—the street bullfight. This was the traditional courtship rite of Terceira. Ask any couple over fifty, and many younger ones, as well, where they met, and the answer will most often be the bullfights. When Maria Elvita was seventeen, it was one of the few places the boys could speak to the girls. But she didn't speak to him that day she first saw him. They looked at each other. She felt she should lower her eyes, but she couldn't look away.

He winked. It was the accepted signal for "May I talk to you later?" She nodded.

That night, he came to the street outside her house and threw pebbles at her window. She didn't go to the window because an older girlfriend told her that you should never appear the first time a boy visited.

The next night, he came on his motorcycle. She went to the window. She couldn't remember now exactly what they talked about. But she remembered telling him her thoughts, when usually her words felt buried, unable to rise out of her throat. She thought he had green eyes. She remembered green eyes. But she couldn't be sure because she was never closer to him than from her window to the street.

He would give her little brother a piece of gum to sit on the veranda and run and warn them if her father was coming. Theirs was still a new, tremulous affection when her father finalized their family's plans to go to America. They had to first take a ferry to São Miguel Island to get on an airplane to California. From the boat, she could see him waving from the dock. He waved until she couldn't see him any longer.

When she got to São Miguel, there was already a letter from him waiting for her. He had written it before she left. Arturo told her he would find her in California.

When they got to California's Central Valley, her family first stayed with her father's sister. To her, the aunt seemed sophisticated. She was a woman who knew about men and life.

The aunt saw the letters that arrived for Maria Elvita.

"Don't be fooled," she told her. "Everyone knew your family had a sponsor. He only sees you as a ticket to America."

Maria Elvita's face stung at the words. She didn't think she was as beautiful as many of the other girls, and she was shy. Now it made sense to her why handsome Arturo had chosen her. She could feel her heart beat in her ears. She ran upstairs and scrawled him a note: "Don't write me any more letters. I know you only see me as your ticket to America."

She went to high school in California. She had a best friend, Mary, who was also a Portuguese immigrant. Mary was sure of herself and always laughing. She liked fashionable clothes, even wearing miniskirts. They cruised the main street of Turlock in Maria Elvita's father's car on Saturday night.

After graduation, Maria Elvita started working at a chicken-processing plant. One day, tired and feeling an aching sadness she couldn't connect to a specific reason, she came home from work and her neighbor, a gossipy woman who sometimes made up her juicy reportings, knocked on the door.

"A man was here looking for you," she said. "He left a message. He said, 'Tell Maria Elvita I didn't need her to get to California. That was never the reason.'"

She kept her face composed in front of the nosy neighbor.

Then she went to her room and cried.

Antone's Poem

Elmano and Albertina had a social calendar as packed as their Catholic church on Sunday. So I was surprised to see their car in the driveway as I passed. I pulled a U-turn with the impetuousness of a true Azorean driver and went to pay a "WOO-woo" visit. Phones have been common in the Azores since the 1970s, but phoning ahead, instead of dropping in, is not.

Elmano was weeding, and Albertina was making cabbage soup. Every counter and table was covered with baskets of produce and plates of pastries dropped off by relatives and friends. It looked as if they were manning a Portuguese deli. Elmano and Albertina were very organized, dutiful, community-minded people, and despite this, I liked them very much.

Albertina, a kindergarten teacher, now had some of the children and grandchildren of her original students as well as new waves of immigrants from California's Central Valley in her class. One little girl came to school dirty and smelling so bad, the other children didn't want to play with her. It was worse than the usual unbathed smell. When Albertina hugged the child, she had to be quite careful not to gag or let show that her eyes watered.

She did what she would do with any student problem: called in the parents to tell them her job was to help them help their child succeed in school.

At that teacher-parent conference, the problem was immediately evident. The young, grateful parents were goat farmers who showed her pictures of the unkempt family and their immaculately groomed goats. Albertina suggested they should read to their daughter every night after bath time—a relaxing bath helped a child retain vocabulary.

The little girl cleaned up only a bit. But for Christmas the parents gave Albertina goat soap.

"Oh, you should have come a few minutes earlier," Albertina said. "Elmano just talked to some people, and they seemed to have some story."

Elmano said he'd noticed three Americans across the street looking lost and gone over. They told them they were looking for the wife's grandmother's house—or was it her grandfather's? Something about Pico Island. I really should have been there what with the way I like to ask questions, he said.

Driving home, I passed three American-looking people at a bus stop. I knew:

1. It was unlikely that any bus would be coming soon.
2. These had to be Elmano's Americans.

I offered Colleen, her husband, Bob, and their daughter, Marie, a ride to their hotel in Angra—provided two of them didn't mind sharing the back seat with wet, stinky Murphy. As Murphy stretched out over the laps of Bob and Marie, better to share his ocean-soaked shedding, I drove up the road behind Altares's sky-blue and white church. Trees arched over the road, touching in the middle to form a sun-dappled tunnel.

I explained we were cutting through the interior of the island, between two volcanoes. As we climbed, Colleen told me that it was a poem written by her great-grandfather Antone that had brought them to the Azores. Tomorrow, early, they were to depart for Pico Island, where Antone was born.

He had an incredible story, she said, just as Barney's temperature gauge spun over to hot. I backed off the gas, hoping to not alarm my passengers, but steam was puffing out of the hood in rolling clouds. I pulled over. We were at the spot where they choose and sort the bulls for the festas. On weekends, families picnic by the pens while little boys play with calves and cows—good practice for someday sharing the street with a bull.

Within minutes of my popping the hood, several cars had pulled over, and there were eleven people who were not mechanics gazing at Barney's engine and nodding. My father, who was a mechanic, used to call this phenomenon "looking at the art."

I called Elmano, and he left a family luncheon to come to rescue the trio of Americans I had now stranded between volcanoes. He used his Portuguese to call a tow company for me.

The crowd dispersed, and Murphy and I settled in to wait. And wait. Shadows lengthened. It grew dark. I got in the back seat and draped a snoring Murphy over my legs like a lap blanket.

The noise of the first crane startled me. A rumble, then a dark shadow passing over the car. I watched as a crate with a loudly bellowing bull was lowered into a pen. That crane had barely dropped off its cargo before two more arrived. Sometimes three or four villages host a fight on the same night. Altogether there are about three hundred *touradas à corda* during the summer. I was stranded at bull central.

There are more cows than year-round people on Terceira, and Murphy had barked at each sad-eyed mellow cow we had ever passed. But he seemed to find the bellowing of bulls melodious and continued to peacefully slumber, while I grew unnerved at the rage-filled echoing chorus.

Elmano called to make sure I had made it home. I could hear the dinner party in full swing behind him. The noble thing was to lie and say all was well and let the poor man enjoy his meal.

I am not that noble.

He arrived to fetch Murphy and me just as the tow truck finally showed up because that's how these things work in all countries.

A month later, I received an email from Colleen with a copy of Antone's poem. In 171 stanzas (yes, 171) he told the story of his life.

"In the year 1863, what a year enormous. / On the 9th of April, I fell into this world," he wrote.

His mother, unmarried and poor, had grieved. She had been deceived by his father, a rich man. She died when Antone was a child. His only memory of her was her crying. As he grew older, people in the village told him he should introduce himself to his father. One day, bringing in firewood, he ran into the man. He told him his mother's name and that he was his son. The man slapped him. It was a slap Antone remembered until his dying day.

> A man who denies his own son
> And calls him a foundling
> Has to answer to God and should not be forgiven.

Antone was taken in by a kind godfather but still left school to go whaling. On one ship he was beaten. Thrown into the water from another. He was shipwrecked for seven months in a remote land where six of the crew died. Eventually, he ended up in California. He married a woman from the Azores. She was Colleen's grandmother, and she grew up in the house across the street from Elmano and Albertina's.

The stanzas that made me wince the most were Antone's vivid recollections of the first whale he helped kill. On September 14, 1879, the ship he was on spotted a whale. He describes the initial lancing. The wounded whale hitting one of four small boats with her tail. Men in the water. Antone saw one drown. A second lancing. The enraged whale fighting back, biting another boat. Everyone in Antone's boat was tossed into water bloody from the whale's wounds. The survivors were rescued and taken back on ship. The next day Antone and the others were ordered back into small boats to go and cut her up.

Colleen's great-grandmother translated Antone's poem into English, and it was passed down to all his descendants. Colleen had read the poem as a little girl.

"It was a sad story and exciting at the same time. For some strange reason, I felt I knew him," Colleen wrote me.

Antone killed himself when he was fifty-four. In Catholicism, suicide is considered a sin and the person who took their life is denied a Catholic burial. Colleen, now with a grown daughter of her own, had come to help put his soul at rest. She and Bob and Marie found the house in Pico where Antone was born and his mother cried.

They went to the church in Magdalena. They prayed for Antone's soul, and Marie, who has a clear, rich voice, sang "Pie Jesu," the medieval requiem for the dead:

> Father, who takes away the sins of the world
> Grant them rest, grant them rest

After reading Colleen's email, I put on my hiking boots and woke up Murphy, who was snoring, all four paws to the ceiling. "Hey, buddy. C'mon, there's somewhere I need to go," I told him, because of course I talk to my dog like a person.

I parked the car at a *miradoura*—scenic turnout—and walked up to a *vigias* that Chef had shown me many years back. It was an open stone turret with a slit. In the whale-hunting days, a man had stood there with a spyglass to the slit and sent a rocket in the air when he spotted a whale. Whaling was once a way of life in the Azores. They stopped hunting whales in these waters in only 1987.

Now, the ocean around the nine islands was one of the largest whale sanctuaries in the world. One-third of all the world's whale and dolphin species pass through, including the occasional California gray whale.

Usually I have the attention span of a gnat, but on this day I was determined to wait. Less than an hour later, I saw what I had come to see: a telltale white spout—then another and another.

I waved to the whales, patted Murphy on the head, and on the walk back recited part of an e. e. cummings poem—the closest thing to a hymn that I have memorized: *i thank You God for most this amazing / day: for the leaping greenly spirits of trees / and a blue true dream of sky; and for everything / which is natural which is infinite which is yes.*

Dancing at Ti Choa

The Azores sit in the middle of the Gulf Stream's warm waters, so even though they're as far north as New York, the weather is never really cold or really hot and there is always moisture in the air. The humidity keeps the hills a rich green and means that a wildfire won't burn, but it can be hard on pudding-headed sorts overly concerned with the texture of their hair. Like me. Redheads are vulnerable to such worries. We're conditioned to believe that there's only a few flyaway hairs' difference between siren and Pippi Longstocking, Little Orphan Annie, or Witchiepoo. Luckily, my allegiance to fighting frizz led to a reunion.

I bumped into Maria Elvita. She asked me about a salon. I whipped out a card my neighbor Mannie had passed on to me from his wife, Mary, since I was researching these things.

Maria Elvita scrunched her face in thought.

"Mannie from Serreta?" she asked. "Why, Mary, his wife, is Mary my best friend from high school. I didn't know they were here."

The four of us planned a night out at Ti Choa, the only restaurant in Serreta. People came from all over the island to eat its traditional Azorean specialties, each involving freshly butchered pig and cow parts. One sister, Lissandra, cooked the *alcatra* and the blood sausages and pork ribs. The other sister, Deluisa, ran the front of the restaurant. I'm the sort of Californian whose favorite meat is a good avocado, but it was a Friday, so I was excited.

On Fridays at Ti Choa, they bake bread in a big wood-burning oven. The first time I tasted this bread, I was chatting along and absent-mindedly broke off a piece and put it in my mouth.

Everything else stopped. My entire attention turned to the bread. The thick brown crust was chewy, the pale soft interior a beehive of bread and pockets of warm air. There was the faintest whisper of sweetness.

The recipe comes from their great-grandmother. It is based on *pão caseiro*, traditional Portuguese home-style bread but with an until-now-secret ingredient: sweet potato yeast.

The bread baking begins early in the afternoon. Deluisa builds a fire burning cedar and clippings from their garden. Smoke comes out of the oven's chimney, and Serreta smells like Christmas in summer. The loaves go into the oven midafternoon. The scent of yeasty goodness wafts through town. You can smell it from the church stairs and over at the Casa de Povo—community center—where the old men are playing cards. When Sergio, Ti Choa's ever-droll waiter, comes in for his shift, he takes the bread out of the oven, and it stays warm under thick towels while he changes clothes and sets the tables.

While we waited outside for the little white restaurant with cheery red window trim to open (in the Azores, restaurant hours are seldom exact), Mannie told us the story of how Ti Choa got its name.

Many years ago, the man who had owned the property left to work in Canada. When he returned, he said "sure"—in English—to everything. He said it with a thick accent: "showa, showa." He became known as Ti Choa. Uncle Sure-a.

When the family first bought the house and were remodeling it for a restaurant, people kept coming by and asking, "What are you doing with Ti Choa's?" So that's what they named the place.

Once we were inside, Sergio put baskets of warm bread on the table and brought a bottle of red wine.

White wine is not always afforded full respect in Portugal. I once biked down the coast of the mainland with a wine aficionado. A waiter recommended a full-bodied red, and my friend said, "Really? But we ordered fish. Not white wine?"

The waiter said, "Sir, in Portugal we believe in good wine. So always red."

Mary looked relaxed. She had been feeling fragile. Over the past few years, she had survived illness and was still so thin, her shoulders were pointy. She'd nursed Mannie through a heart attack and had a scare when their youngest grandson almost died of an odd, random infection.

Everyone was well now, and Mary had been crumbling with anxiety because she finally could. A man was playing an electric piano. There was live music on bread nights. Mannie asked Mary to dance. They swirled in the little space between tables, and everyone watched and smiled.

Back in California, Mannie had staged his own dating service to find her.

He'd dated some American-born, non-Portuguese girls but felt marriage would take him too far from his culture. On the other hand, when he first arrived in California, even at the age of ten, what he liked best were all the bare female legs.

"I couldn't see myself with one of those fresh-off-the-boat girls swaddled neck to ankle," he said.

He asked one of his friends if there were any "greenies"—new immigrants—at school.

"There is this one girl, Mary, but all the boys like her," she said.

"How does she dress?" he asked.

"She dresses nice," his friend told him. "Fashionable. She even wears short skirts."

Mannie begged her to set up a double date. He was immediately smitten by the lively Mary. He was determined to see her again. But she was from a traditional family and wouldn't be allowed to go out on a date alone. He made plans to come back the next weekend to see her at, of course, a bullfight. She would be there with her aunt and cousins.

The California Azoreans couldn't successfully import the *touradas à corda* because they didn't have towns with narrow streets and Portuguese-style houses to send a bull down. So they imported and grew that other Azorean bullfighting tradition: *forçado.*

Forçado bullfighting may exist just to keep *tourada à corda* from seeming too dangerous and loony. Eight men wearing skintight breeches, lacy white knee socks, red cummerbunds, cropped brocade jackets, and the sort of long woolen hats favored by elves line up single file.

The guy at the front of the line—the *caras*—walks ahead to "call" the bull, making eye contact, yelling, *"Touro! Touro!"* and stamping his foot if that's what it takes. When the bull charges, the *caras* backpedals. If all goes well, the bull, its horns wrapped in leather, will hit him smack in the gut, then plow through the rest of the line, piling up *forçados* like meringue ripples.

Portuguese immigrants come from all over California to go to one of these bullfights. I had witnessed three thousand people at the ring in tiny Stevinson.

Which was about the scene when Mannie arrived at the bullfight where he was to see Mary. He was late. He'd had to finish school, work at a dairy, and then drive two hours. The stands were packed, but he was sure he could spot her. When that didn't work, he tried standing in a conspicuous spot for Mary to spot him. That didn't work either.

The man announcing the bullfight was a friend of his father's. Mannie got the idea to have Mary paged.

A security guard—a big, beefy guy—wouldn't let him pass. Incensed, Mannie went to the outside of the rickety stands and climbed two stories' worth of jungle gym construction to get to the announcer.

Over the loudspeaker, the man asked Mary to meet Mannie at the beer garden.

When she got there, Mary was furious. Why, people were going to think she drank beer!

Eventually, they both calmed down, and they have been married nearly half a century.

I asked Maria Elvita whether she had seen Arturo, the man from her youth. She said Elmano had heard he was married, if it was the same man.

"But wouldn't it be nice to say hello, even if he is married?" I asked her. "Do you think his wife is going to be bothered by something from fifty years ago?"

Mary cocked her head and tightened her lips. "You never know," she said.

I felt oddly invested in Maria Elvita's talking to Arturo.

I was at the point where I figured my grand romances were behind me. But I wanted to believe that they mattered.

We have this one life. But all the roads not taken, all those other lives we might have lived, are a part of it too. Yearning—that terrible, beautiful gaping yawn of want for a person, a place, a chance, a change, or something we can't name—leaves craters, spaces for us to hold more of life. *Saudade* might be a strictly Portuguese word, but aching want is a universal condition.

"I could find him, you know," I told Maria Elvita. "I'm a reporter, and there are about as many people on this whole island as there are in Trader Joe's on a busy night."

Mary and Mannie looked alarmed. In that unspoken way of things, I knew that they thought I didn't know that Maria Elvita had fought alcoholism and been through a divorce and might be chasing ghosts.

But it was Terceira. I knew the rough outlines of her life without her telling me.

It wasn't gossip in the usual sense. (Although there was plenty of that. I'd felt like the stalked subject of paparazzi the first time I was on the island, my every move logged by watching eyes.) This was something else. People often filled you in, very matter-of-factly with no added commentary, on the essential facts of someone's life. Whose dad died when they were twelve. Whose mother committed suicide, causing them to postpone their wedding. Who didn't speak to his brother for ten years. I'd once mentioned to Chef, my cultural translator, this constant morbid litany.

"It's not morbid," he said. "Remember, it is a small island, and for many generations we must all live together all our lives, so it is the habit to always pass down the knowledge that would make us—how would you say?—cut each other some slack."

I'd barely met Maria Elvita, but I could see how she might want to go back to a young love she'd thrown over because of insecurities and say, "I grew into a stronger woman than that." If for no other reason than to remind herself it was true.

São Jorge Cheese

Elmano and Albertina always spoke about having a mixed marriage. They were both Azoreans. But they were from different islands. They split each summer between his family home on Terceira and hers on São Jorge.

They invited me to visit them on Albertina's island despite my having Murphy. Albertina was afraid of dogs. She'd been bitten as a child. But she'd slowly gotten accustomed to Murphy, and they had a tentative relationship.

The ferry ride over was troublesome. Murphy had to travel in a crate on the lower deck with the Vespas and the luggage. He was displeased. He howled. But Murphy doesn't really have a howl. It's more a deep-throated cackle. I've always thought it sounded a little like a rooster's call. But many people on board thought it sounded a little like engine trouble. I was allowed to go below and keep Murphy company. It was against the rules, but the crew deemed it better than mass anxiety.

When we got to Albertina's family home, she gave Murphy a small pat on his big head, which required courage on her part. We were on the veranda with a sweeping view of the sea, and Murphy started "talking" to Albertina. He carried on with a series of rumbles and whines. Apparently he had discovered his verbal abilities on the ferry and planned to keep using them.

"What's he saying?" Albertina asked, looking alarmed.

"I wish I knew," I told her. "But I'm sure it's something funny."

They took me for a tour around a zucchini of an island that was thirty-three miles long and five miles at its widest point. Our first stop was the most photographed spot in the Azores—a view of cliffs, crashing waves, and hills of hydrangeas with huge pom-poms of lavender-blue blooms. The flowers weren't native, but after arriving from Southeast Asia or the Americas, they had become so ubiquitous that they were now the icon of the islands.

We stopped at a factory near Beira that sold cheese.

Wait. I can already hear a chorus of censure from Azoreans. Let me rephrase. Not cheese—São Jorge cheese. *Old* São Jorge cheese.

Eight traditional cheese makers are part of a cooperative that produces São Jorge cheese. In 1986, they obtained PDO—protected designation origin. It's like the dairy-goods version of French champagne. The island's economy revolves around this strong-smelling semihard cheese. Its history goes back to fifteenth-century Flemish settlers who brought their cheese-making ways. Old wooden sailing ships once stopped here to load up on wheels for ocean voyages. It's a combination of raw cow's milk from the morning and evening milkings. The whey they use for the culture comes from the batch before it—so a cheese may have a pungent lineage that stretches back hundreds of years. The São Jorge cheeses sold throughout the Azores and through some international shops are three months, seven months, or one year old. For the really strong stuff, you have to go to São Jorge.

Elmano and Albertina were always prepared. They had a big ice chest in the back for the cheese they were going to buy. They had ordered ahead. Of course, they knew Mary Lou, the woman helping us—oh, and her children's names, the date of her anniversary, and how she'd met her husband. They saw her here every year. She pulled out their fifteen-pound wheel. With the flair and solemnity of a sommelier, she cut three small slivers.

Elmano and Albertina nodded pleasantly at the taste. I carefully unglued my tongue from the roof of my mouth, where it had retreated from the cheese's sting.

Mary Lou leaned forward and conspiratorially whispered, "This is one and a half years old. Or we have one three-year-old cheese. I saved it for you, just in case."

Elmano nodded yes. Albertina met my eyes and raised her eyebrows.

I've never gone shopping for jewels, but I would imagine it's something like watching the unveiling of a three-year-old São Jorge cheese. The respect, the ceremony, the excitement of someone waving off the lesser baubles and asking to see what is in the vault. We each took a sliver. I'm glad I watched Elmano before trying mine so that I didn't miss any of his reaction, which went in this order:

Widening of eyes in surprise.

One high-pitched little "hmph."

Then a full-on giggle.

There was no other word for it. It was a gurgle of pure delight. He was the banker in *Mary Poppins* learning to fly a kite.

I tried my sliver. It really was amazing how much violence could be set off in one mouth by one little piece of cheese: thousands of pinpricks, odd vibrations. My eyes watered. It was fun.

I knew there were rivalries between islands, so I hadn't paid much mind when people would tell me *their* island was the most beautiful. All nine were volcanic, green, and plop in the middle of the Atlantic. I figured it was like picking the cutest dog in a litter of Murphy-clone Lab puppies.

But São Jorge startled me. From the ferry it looked like a towering emerald fortress ringed by waterfalls. It was a steep, secretive island. The main villages were on the tops of cliffs. Hairpin roads went down to the *fajãs*—sea-level capes that had formed when lava flowed out to the ocean and cooled and cliffs had crumbled down.

In the old days, people lived on top most of the year and moved down to the *fajãs* during the wine harvest and ensuing festas. Now some were deserted and some had small year-round populations that swelled each summer with returning emigrants and the sort of surfers who chased waves to remote spots around the world.

About ten thousand people lived on São Jorge full-time, and there were twenty thousand cows. The pastures were even higher than the villages, and above them were woods of giant ferns and species of trees that may have survived the Ice Age.

In Albertina's *fajã* far below the main road, red-tile houses spilled over hillsides that sloped to a little port. A short hike led to lava-rock pools that made Biscoitos look like bath time. These were ringed by towering, ropy black walls, the stone in the shapes of candle drippings. It took a daring dive or a climb down a long red ladder to reach the water. There were underwater caves filled with swirling surf, and the tides in the pools tugged and surged. There were no sunbathing crowds or anywhere flat to put them. Even Murphy had trouble climbing out of the water on algae-slick boulders.

Saint George was said to have slayed dragons. So, adding to the fairy-tale feel of the island was the repeated motif of dragons and saints. They were in the patterns of the cobblestones in the two port towns, embroidered on pot holders and dish towels.

My stay was two days, just long enough to look around and think that if a person was going to tell another person to come on over and attempt a romantic interlude, Albertina's *fajã* might be the place.

The final night, after dinner at the one restaurant in Albertina's village, we ordered passion fruit mousse and drank more wine. I found myself wondering about Elmano and Albertina's relationship. He had his arm around her chair. If he made a joke, she laughed and said, "Oh, Elman!" shortening his name.

I'd always considered stable, task-oriented unions like theirs the opposite of romance.

They'd met during her first year teaching kindergarten. He was on his way to being a principal at a different school. There was no wild serendipity. It was the careful courtship of two people of similar good character. I knew they led marriage workshops at their Catholic church.

"So what makes you guys so pro marriage?" I asked, being given to regarding it as a suspect institution. "Do you think it's just your culture, tradition?"

With almost as much enthusiasm as he'd shown for the cheese, Elmano shook his head no. "I can't imagine having lived my life without Albertina," he said. "She really is my best friend." This from the man who joked in front of Albertina about the less demanding wife he'd find if she died first.

Albertina looked off, thinking for a moment. "It's the thing that makes everything else worth it," she said.

"So what do you teach people in those marriage classes?" I asked. "What are the tips?"

"One thing is we spend most of our time with couples who like each other," Elmano said. "Being around people who don't like being married to each other can be contagious."

"I better be careful around you two, then," I joked. "Maybe it works the other way."

I told them I had a friend—maybe more than a friend—who wanted to visit from California. They thought it might be a good idea.

The next morning, before I caught the ferry, Albertina, Murphy, and I took a walk. Albertina even held Murphy's leash. The gate of the prettiest house in the *fajã*—the two-story one with a walled garden right next to a small rocky beach—was open.

"WOO-woo, Eduardo," Albertina called.

The man who came out from the side of the house had sky-blue eyes and a wave of white hair. He was at least in his seventies, wearing a white shirt with flowing sleeves and frayed, melon-colored pants tucked into the sort of knee boots that Azorean dairy farmers wear. If the man himself did not bring to mind a romantic figure of an artist—there was all the art.

His yard was filled with sculptures of mermaids covering their breasts with their hands, jumping dolphins, and bejeweled tortoises. A prince in a crown and goatee bore a striking resemblance to Eduardo, only black haired and youthful. There were men plowing with oxen, Catholic saints, and fantastical creatures, as well as the whales and dolphins that frequent the Azores. The hair and jewels and decorations of the simple sculptures were formed with small black rocks from the beach in front of the house. Their style was simple and folkloric but singular. The sculptures lived between patterned walkways, flower gardens, and hanging grapevines. He had carved the dates into pieces, and it was clear that he had been at this at least twenty years.

Eduardo picked some grapes and offered them to us. With Albertina translating, I learned that Eduardo had never studied art. But during a few years in Italy, where he was working a manufacturing job to make money, he had taught himself how to cast and carve. He had never shown his work or tried to show his work. He harbored no dream, he said, of being discovered. His art was something he did only because he had "a feeling of the need to do it."

I asked which was his favorite piece, although I had a feeling I already knew what he would say. And he did.

"It is always the piece I am going to start next," he said.

From São Jorge, in the center of the archipelago, there were views of other islands on all sides: Pico, Faial, Graciosa, and Terceira.

There's a much-quoted line by Portuguese writer Raul Brandão: *"Já percebi que o que torna as ilhas belas e as completa é a ilha em frente"*—"I have come to understand that what makes the islands beautiful and complete is the island that's across the way." Maybe life is like that. For all our talk about living in the moment, what makes the present beautiful and complete is also imagining what we will do next.

Good Riddance, Barney

You know those days when you feel right with the world, comfortable in your own skin, ready to meet the gaze of strangers with cheer and inquisitiveness?

I wasn't having one of those days.

I was back on Terceira. Barney wouldn't start. Again. This time it was my fault. Despite the pink and yellow Post-it notes I had plastered across my dashboard with reminders—"*Luzes do carro!*"—I had left the car lights on. (As with everything else on Barney, the warning chime did not work.) I was trudging up the hill to the mechanic's shop to ask whether they would come to jump-start my car.

Up ahead, a couple got out of a Jeep. The man was tall, with a shock of sandy hair falling in his eyes and dimples. Not Portuguese. The woman had dark, curly hair. Purple toenail polish that matched purple-accented Teva sandals. Maybe Portuguese. I'd guess someone's American granddaughter.

I nodded a quick hello that didn't invite conversation. I wasn't in the mood to talk to anyone.

My bad mood had started the evening before, when Murphy found yet another cow-water tank to take a swim in. This one was the worst yet of a summer of pulling my dog out of slimy cisterns where he tried to catch frogs. I dragged him back, definitively green and with tiny translucent worms wiggling all over him.

Before Murphy discovered frog diving, there had been blissful hours of wandering free over pastures, climbing old wooden gates, and following hedges of hydrangeas. Murphy would race over the hills, a leaping blur of white against green grass and blue sea.

I kept thinking that I felt like a Welsh poet but couldn't quite recall why I thought that, until one day I found some Wi-Fi and searched "Welsh poet." Once I saw Dylan Thomas's name, I could picture his "Fern Hill" poem printed with a woodcut illustration in an old, cloth-covered book with some name like *One Hundred Classic Poems* that I'd had as a child.

And as I was green and carefree, famous among the barns . . .

I'd been reading lately that society was moving away from written literary to visual communication. I couldn't fathom not having words from different ages and places rattling in the recesses of my mind, allowing me to identify with a Welsh poet, even if I didn't remember all of his poem.

These days, my ramblings weren't so poetic. Every time I let Murphy off his leash, he ran for dank cattle water. After hosing him off the night before, I had walked straight into a shower. I got out, flashed again in my mind to translucent worms, and took another shower.

And one more.

It still seemed a miracle to me that I could take all the showers I wanted to. There was no need to conserve water. In California the drought continued, and every shower there was a luxury.

My three-shower frizzed hair was piled atop my head in a style usually associated with Pebbles Flintstone. My clothes were dirty because the landlord said I would have access to a laundry room in the big house, but it was booked with a never-ending stream of international honeymooners. Hooray for love and all of that, but it got in my way when I wanted to do a load of socks. Plus, Serreta was often damp and gray on days when the rest of the island was blue and sunny. Like today. It was like being the only one not invited to the party.

Truth was, I was feeling a little melancholy. I missed Romana and John and that other summer. I missed Chef the way he used to be. I missed me the way I used to be. I even missed longing instead of feeling done with everything.

I turned off the main road and up the steep lane to the shop. So did the couple. This was odd. It was very out-of-the-way. It was getting awkward walking up a narrow Azorean lane and not starting a conversation with two likely fellow Americans.

"My car's battery is dead," I finally said, nodding at the mechanic's shop.

"We're thinking of buying out my dad and the other relatives for my grandmother's house," the woman said, nodding at the house directly across the street. She told me to come over if I wanted after I was done talking to Selio (she knew the mechanic's name).

I did. Their names were Chris and Delcione, and they showed me the generations of family photos on the walls and the bunk beds the grandparents had bought for Delcione and her sister—when they were in their twenties. The Bostonian sisters had spent every childhood summer in the Azores. Delcione remembers walking the cow home from pasture when she was five.

Chris and Delcione had been married eleven years, but Delcione's father was still always introducing Delcione to eligible Azoreans.

"With me standing right there," Chris said, shaking his head.

He was from Michigan. He'd left the small town he grew up in and moved to Boston to work for a steel company just before the 9/11 attacks.

"I'd never been so alone in my life, and then the world blew up," he said.

His office became a frantic place. Dave, an Azorean guy in the office who lived with his parents and siblings and was constantly among a gaggle of cousins he'd known his whole life, was astounded at a guy all alone. He took Chris under his wing, inviting him home for dinner and to Portuguese festas.

Chris, it turned out, was to an Azorean family what I was to an Armenian one.

Chris was envious of Dave's ties. Dave was envious of Chris's freedom. He started showing up at work with an overnight bag on Fridays so he could crash at Chris's apartment on weekends. Soon Chris had an unofficial roommate, and as far as Dave's mother was concerned, she had a new son.

Each year in Boston there's what is unofficially known as the Luso Booze Cruise. *Luso* is a term that refers to all Portuguese speakers. (Lusitania was a name for the Iberian Peninsula during the time of the Roman Empire.) But the history of the area's Portuguese population stretches back to the days of whaling in the Azores. So in Boston, a Luso Booze Cruise meant, specifically, drunk Azoreans. Dave invited Chris to the cruise but then didn't show.

Chris remembered a bunch of Portuguese guys giving the one decidedly non-Portuguese guy looks you wouldn't exactly call welcoming. Delcione was stood up for the same cruise by her sister Nivia.

Chris and Delcione had met before in gatherings of Dave's extended Azorean circles. But the cruise was the first time they really talked.

Delcione recalled thinking, *Wow, so this is what a man who isn't a chauvinist is like.* At the time, she was dating a traditional Italian American, which was acceptable to her father, she said, "because if your daughter doesn't marry Portuguese, Italian is the next-closest thing. Both cultures let the man think he is the king."

Chris thought he knew even from that early conversation that they would marry, but he also remembered thinking, *Never. She's out of my league.*

Anyway, the thing about the cruise that would bring them closer together was the two people who weren't there.

A couple of months after the cruise, Delcione and Nivia went to Angra with their Boston folkloric Azorean group. Nivia wasn't as much fun as usual. She didn't want to go out. She wasn't drinking.

She was pregnant. The father wasn't her longtime boyfriend.

Ever since she was a little girl, Nivia had had a crush on Chris's friend Dave. She told Delcione that during festa preparations in the church that year, she had looked at Dave and then marched over and told him how she felt.

Dave had been shocked. She was like a little sister to him.

"Obviously," said Delcione, "he recovered from his shock. My sister is really beautiful."

"I don't know," said Chris. "I look back now and remember how weird he'd been acting. He was a little shell-shocked."

"I still can't believe either of them could keep a secret," Delcione said, laughing.

There was a tense family dinner when Nivia told her father he was going to be a grandfather. He looked at Delcione.

"Don't look at me!" Delcione exclaimed. Her father had always pegged her as the rebel. When she was little, she told him she wanted to marry an Azorean and stay in the islands all year. He told her that only the worst player in the Serreta marching band would marry her because she was too independent. Even back then, her father had probably resigned himself to an Italian American son-in-law, but she didn't think he'd ever imagined a white guy from Michigan.

At Dave and Nivia's wedding, Delcione and Chris reunited and a first date became a long weekend, and they've been a couple ever since.

We were now in the dining room of the house that had belonged to her grandmother, and all of us were staring at a large porcelain figure on the table. It was about three feet tall. It had the face of a monkey but pale, with large green eyes and exaggerated swoops of black lashes. Swirls and swirls of yellow, meant to suggest either cake frosting or fur or possibly flowers, sat atop its head and above its paws. In its mouth the seated creature held a nosegay of flowers in a pale-blue basket.

"A poodle?" I suggested uncertainly.

"A lion? A lamb?" Chris countered.

"A tisket, a tasket, an ugly thing with a basket," Delcione sang. She looked at Chris. "I'm sorry, honey, but it's here to stay. It's part of the place—I ain't lion," she said.

"I don't know, let me lamb-ent about it," he said.

It was my first encounter with what would become evident during weeks of hanging out with Chris and Delcione: they were punsters. It wasn't that I equated punning with, say, a plush-toy sexual fetish. It was just that same sort of surprise to discover Chris and Delcione were into wordplay.

It was like when I was a waitress in Palm Springs, California, which hosts a lot of kinky conventions. The restaurants would get a list of what groups were in town, and it was always interesting to note that the Mennonite Women's Quilting Group was booked the same week as the Inland Empire Spankers or some such. I would wait on a table of middle-aged couples in Bermuda shorts and polo golf shirts and then check the list and be a little shocked to find their plastic wristbands meant they were the same people who would be stripping down and paddling strangers later.

On my walk home, the sun came out—even in Serreta. Talking with Chris and Delcione was instantly rat-a-tat familiar (other than the punning—that was a new one). I felt less lonely.

The mechanic, Selio (who was in business with his brother Delio), drove over but couldn't start Barney. He put in a new battery and I handed him another seventy euros.

The week before, I had finally paid for the car.

Mariza at the store had tried to persuade me not to hand over the cash. She had made choppy zigzags in the air with her finger, bobbed her head back and forth like those toy dogs people used to put in the back window of their car, and glared like a feminist icon while enacting how I should say, “No way am I paying full price for a car you had to have known was a piece of crap.” But, alas, a deal is a deal, and besides, Elmano was involved, and even though I tried the finger-and-head thing in the mirror later, it was abundantly clear I was no Mariza.

Elmano and I met up with the man married to Elmano’s cousin’s wife’s sister and his business partner—a.k.a. a friend from junior high and a brother-in-law with a shared fashion sense. They were both wearing bright orange shirts, though slightly different shades. It was clear they were bold, entrepreneurial spirits. The municipal office where we transferred ownership of Barney was also the place to get divorces. The business partner said it was a good place to find women who had a new need for a gardener (he had a side business) or couples who wanted to sell a car or a house fast. Barney seemed to have been one of a fleet.

As we walked to the insurance office, the not-quite-a-relative-of-Elmano told me I had gotten a great deal. “All the Americans want automatic transmission,” he said. “You’ll be able to sell that car easy!”

“I think I have a car for life,” I snapped, stealing Chef’s line. “Because no one but me would ever buy that car.”

He looked wounded.

I felt bad.

Then I got home and found out he was right.

I was throwing Murphy and a beach towel into Barney’s back seat. A big truck pulled up, and a woman on the passenger side hollered, “I heard you had an American car you might want to sell.”

“You wouldn’t want to buy this,” I told her. “It’s been nothing but trouble.”

“No, I would,” she said, getting out of the truck.

Jeanette, who had grown up in Artesia, said she came over every summer with her two young daughters. Her husband had to keep working in California. She stayed with her mother-in-law and had to ask her brother-in-law to drive her places, and she didn't drive stick shift, and she *really* wanted her own car. (I could see how she might feel like that.)

"But what if it breaks down on you all the time?" I asked.

"No problem," she said. "My husband's brother can fix anything."

She was leaving soon. She had to get back to the Central Valley because her oldest daughter was a festa princess and would be making the circuit of the celebrations there. She said that if I sold her the car, I could drive it the rest of my stay and she'd have it waiting for her the next summer.

She offered €1,200. I agreed. I could see her daughters in the truck wearing matching pink swimming suits. The ends of their hair were pink from their beautician mother dipping them in Kool-Aid. I offered them a ride, and we all went to the lava-rock pools.

Jeanette waded in the water, talking to her husband on the phone, telling him she'd bought a car in the Azores like a car they'd once owned in California. Maybe the car would work out for her—at this point it had many new parts. The girls took turns throwing a stick into the water for Murphy. Good riddance, Barney.

The Impérios

Despite looking like a couple from one of those outdoor adventure catalogs, Chris and Delcione had no interest in outdoor adventure. I spent the mornings hiking with Murphy and sticking to my mission of sniffing flowers and listening to birds and oohing and aahing over trees, to counter my apocalyptic visions of drought and fires and floods. Then I met up with Chris and Delcione to sit and sip under various café umbrellas.

It reminded me of sitting in Odie and Armen's backyard and drinking tea and pondering life, which always reminded Odie of doing the same in an Iranian courtyard. Delcione said she knew she would think about these afternoons when they were back in Boston, even though she'd be too busy to think. We'd fallen into the grown-up version of summer camp friends, freely and instantly sharing the details of our life. They knew about Moody and his new nickname: Endicott.

Jack Moody was no saccharine, candy-proffering suitor. But when Moody told his group of guy friends—including his best friend, a cat-loving gambler who often had his hand on the steering wheel of his Buick and his bookie on the phone, and his brother, who felt the only form of true love was between a man and his hunting dog—of his desire to visit me in the Azores, they nicknamed him Endicott from an old Kid Creole and the Coconuts song about a goody-two-shoes, attentive beau. They were like a middle-aged version of boys with a "No Girls

Allowed" sign. I was still surprised Moody was ready to venture from the clubhouse.

Chris thought the nickname Endicott was very funny and also a sign that this was a good guy waiting for me to give the go-ahead. This day's alcohol-infused debate was about what I was waiting for.

"The problem is there was someone from Portugal that I'm not sure I'll ever be really over," I said.

"Wait!" Chris shouted (I mentioned the alcohol). "Endicott knows there was a guy from Europe?!"

I nodded yes, not understanding the shock. Moody and I had known each other more than a dozen years with no reason to keep secrets. There wasn't a lot we didn't know.

"You don't understand," Chris said. "Us American guys, we have a thing about European dudes. We think we can't compete. They have thousands of years of romance behind them. They have Casanova; we have Davy Crockett. Endicott is my hero!"

Chris had bona fides in the broken-heart-and-moving-on department. Before he met Delcione, he'd walked in on his best friend having sex with his live-in fiancée. (How many times have I heard similar stories? Lock the door, people. No one needs that in their memory banks.) Chris told me that every once in a while, he still thought of that moment. "And when I do, I think, *Yes! Thank God. Or I wouldn't be married to Del*," he had told me, pumping his fist in the air.

He had a point. Utter betrayal leaves you free in a way that mutually losing your way doesn't.

But a friend of mine whose husband died has a theory that there are four chambers in the human heart—so even if one belongs for eternity to someone missing, there is still room for love. I had to smile thinking of my dad's less poetic version of the sentiment: "A three-legged dog runs plenty fast."

I needed to be sure because if I climbed that ladder, I was jumping. No sad Fiesta Village Waterslide backward climb down.

It was Chris and Delcione's last week in Terceira, so we roused ourselves for a genuine outing. We circled the entire island and looked at many of the *impérios*—small, elaborately decorated chapels whose upkeep belonged to the Cult of the Holy Spirit, a fellowship made up of local families. There are more than fifty *impérios* on the island. At least one in every village—usually right across the street from a Catholic church. The pint-size temples are topped with a crown and a dove and trimmed in distinctive colors. One blue and yellow and red, another green and pink, a couple of them bright turquoise. There are *impérios* painted in yellows and even shades of orange. With their busy architecture and bright hues, they look like a cross between a wedding cake and a piñata.

Each spring the *impérios* come alive as the center of Holy Spirit festivals. It's a celebration in which huge pots of soup and baskets of bread are served, a reminder to practice charity. The chapels are covered with fresh flowers, and each village forms a procession with young girls dressed as queens in white dresses and capes, men carrying medieval flags, and some people carrying baskets of bread on their heads. It's the tradition most closely tied to Azorean identity, and it's embraced with passion by the diaspora. In California, every spring weekend, somewhere in a Portuguese community, they are dishing out free soup. It's a deeply spiritual rite but not a Catholic one, something seldom realized.

Historians believe the Holy Spirit tradition began with Joachim, a monk born in Calabria circa 1135. He was the abbot of a monastery in Fiore, Italy. He came to believe that the Trinity—the Father, Son, and Holy Ghost—represented different ages for humanity. The age of the Father was in the past, they were living in the age of the Son, and ahead was the age of the Holy Spirit, according to Joachim's reading of Scripture. He foretold that in this new era there would be no separation between everyday life and the sacred. The Empire of the Holy Spirit would bring peace, justice, equality, and tolerance. The idea of such a utopia on earth took hold with many people, including Dante, who placed Joachim in paradise in his *Divine Comedy*.

But if ordinary people could communicate directly with the divine, then there wouldn't be a need for the church hierarchy. His teachings were eventually declared heresy. Holy Spirit festivals were stamped out across Europe. But small pockets of resistance remained, notably among Franciscan brotherhoods and the Order of the Knights Templar. (They really existed—they're not just an Indiana Jones plot device.) The king and queen of Portugal were devotees of the Holy Spirit but also very obedient Catholics. They envisioned the church remaining in power forever and recruited groups of laypeople to run the festivals as something separate and not a threat to the established religion. The papacy left them alone, and in Portugal the celebrations continued. The ceremony involved crowning an ordinary person emperor of the Holy Spirit Kingdom. At first the crown had a cross—a symbol of the church and the age of the Son. But it was later replaced by a dove, the symbol of the Holy Spirit and a new age.

Through all that, the Azores remained uninhabited. They were settled by the Portuguese in the 1400s under the management of the Knights of the Order of Christ, the successor to the Knights Templar. Franciscans were among the first to arrive, and they promoted forming cults—or fellowships—of families to organize Holy Spirit festivals.

The colorful chapels we visited on our self-styled tour were remnants of a heretical utopian vision brought to virgin shores. But that wasn't what Delcione and I found most interesting. We were fascinated by the folklore holding that during the Spanish Inquisition, the Holy Spirit Cult offered Jews a way to hide in plain sight.

We both felt a personal connection. For separate and, in my case, maybe spurious reasons, Delcione and I each thought we were a descendant of Sephardic Jews.

Delcione's great-grandfather was born in Serreta on January 6—Three Kings' Day, or Little Christmas, a Christian feast day celebrating the three wise men's visit to baby Jesus. Because of this, the family changed their name to Reis—King. But Delcione said there had long been family whispers that the real reason for the name change was that it was a tradition their family had first started in order to hide Jewish roots.

In 1497 Portugal's Jews were forced to convert, leave the country, or be killed. The forced converts were called New Christians and took new names. As the Spanish Inquisition grew ever more murderous and widespread, they kept changing family names and took multiple surnames for protection. Some families continued the practice for generations.

Jewish people had been among the first Azoreans. In Terceira, one of the first bays claimed by Portugal is called Porto Judeu. The story goes that the Jewish crew member who first swam to shore was given naming privileges. The Azores were again a place of escape for Jewish families during World War II. Research around the Y chromosome of Azoreans showed 13.4 percent of the population have DNA markers common to Jewish origin.

These were enough clues for Delcione and her aunt to give each other DNA tests for Christmas presents (they bought them with a Groupon). The tests revealed Jewish heritage. Now they give each other tiny menorahs at Christmas—only partially to watch Delcione's very Catholic father sputter.

I had less evidence of lineage. I don't know for sure; my ethnicity and I didn't get in on the Groupon deal. As a child, I was bothered that I didn't look like any particular group of people. I had no tribe.

However, during my first visit to the Azores, Chef and I had gone to a museum show about the Spanish Jewish diaspora's history in the islands. There was a painting of an unidentified Sephardic Jewish woman. It wasn't even in a realistic style, more like a painted mosaic. But she had a thin face, a pointy chin, almond-shaped brown eyes, red hair, and spindly arms and legs. Before I could even process my own reaction, Chef gasped and said, "Dear God, she looks just like you."

I had quickly decided that this exhaustive genealogy research (bumping into a painting of someone who generally looked like me) cleared up why I felt so deeply drawn to the Azores. (It's in my blood!) I have thought about a DNA test. But I don't like the idea, because I think it shouldn't matter. I'm a proponent of a one-race sorting system: human. Of course, Del was using the test to prove the same point to her father.

We were talking about all this when Chris suggested that we take a tour of sights of interest to our possible shared heritage. Stopping along the way, of course, to eat fish and let Murphy swim. At each *império*, we made a game of looking at the busy decorations, trying to spot designs that could be interpreted as Hebrew words, a menorah, a Star of David.

One theory was that the *impérios* had been a place that outwardly converted but where secretly practicing Jewish families could meet and practice their faith's rites. Maybe they even incorporated Jewish iconology into the ceremonies and buildings.

Delcione said she thought it was simply a way families forced from their faith and everything familiar could feel comfortable being part of the community.

"Like, Jesus just wasn't their guy, right? But the Holy Spirit was something they knew," she said. "They could get into that."

If the symbols were there, would it matter? Some schools of thought held that even if we don't consciously know the meaning of symbols, they are a way that humans pass down stories told on a different level from words. That seemed fitting to me on an island where so many different legends and myths were always simmering just below the surface. The way people talked about a conversation with someone dead as if they'd just bumped into them at the store could get confusing unless you just let go of strictly linear expectations.

Along with visiting the *impérios*, we took every turnoff that appealed to us. We watched kids run and jump off port walls into the ocean. We snapped photos at a particularly pretty Catholic chapel and followed rutted dirt roads through cow pastures—and we still circled the island in a single afternoon.

That night was the Praia Festa, second in size only to Sanjoaninas at the beginning of the summer. Before I left for the party, I called Endicott—excuse me, I mean, Moody. It made me late to meet Chris and Delcione, and I got stuck behind a children's parade full of Little Mermaids and *Madagascar* penguins.

Chris held a beer high in the air to give me something to aim for as I wedged out of cartoonville and navigated a dancing crowd. He handed it to me like a prize when I got there.

"So," he said by way of greeting. "What did you decide to do about Endicott?"

"I told him to come over," I told Chris, and we clinked our beer bottles in the air.

Chef's band, Ti-Notas, still one of Terceira's (and my) favorite bands, was playing. I always thought it was funny that Chef, the tallest guy onstage, played the *cavaquinho*—the smallest guitar, the ancestor of the ukulele. The Portuguese had brought the instrument to Hawaii. The band also included guitars, drums, a violin, and a lead singer. It was so good to see Chef singing and dancing with his friends. Their music was exuberant, and people locked arms and twirled on this balmy, starry night. One woman was dancing with her baby in a carriage.

Chef, who didn't like to sit still or be alone, had once told me he was glad he was Azorean so he could play music. In the Azores, they pass out instruments to kids in elementary school, and the children learn their instruments together as they learn to play as a band. Chef said if he'd had to be locked away alone to practice like an American kid, he would have never played a note. When music students got older, the ones who really loved their instruments would practice alone to become real musicians. But everyone who grew up on the island could play a little bit of something.

After the concert, a big group of us drank beers on the sidewalk and told stories. Just in this little group there was every example of the vagaries of human migrations.

Before the first time I'd met Chef's best friend, the band's cofounder, Chef had described him as "the most Azorean man I know." Then when he made the introduction, he said, "Diana, this is Jerry." A decidedly non-Portuguese name. Jerry's parents had immigrated to Canada for a brief time when they were young and decided it wasn't for them. But during their stay, they had developed a passion for reruns of Jerry Lewis movies.

Later, at seventeen, Jerry moved to Canada to make his fortune. He stayed with relatives. One evening the Holy Spirit Festa from Angra was on the television on the Portuguese station.

His aunts and uncles and cousins were watching and weeping.

"It was the first time I really understood *saudade*," he said. "And I thought, *Uh-uh—not for me. I'm not going to spend my life longing for my island.*"

The next week there was a concert in Terceira that he wanted to see. He bought a ticket for the concert and a plane ticket and came back to stay.

Stat, the virtuoso violinist, was American born with an American passport. His parents had brought him back as a toddler. He spoke only Portuguese. On a trip to Boston, he showed his passport and then was pulled into an immigration office for hours when he couldn't answer simple questions in English. They told Stat they were sending him back to Portugal before finally releasing him. This happened during a trip with the marching band from the little village of Raminho.

Delcione asked him where they had stayed in Boston, and he started describing the brownstone. Her eyes grew round. "Do you remember what your bedroom looked like?"

He started to describe the bedspread and curtains.

"That's my father's house," she said. "You slept in my bed!"

I was thinking how everyone in the band had relatives in the States or Canada, when I remembered a connection I had forgotten. Tiago, one of the drummers, was related to Romana. He was the one who warned me too many martinis could lead to her speaking Italian. I told him that I kept driving by Romana's house, waiting for her to arrive. He said she'd grown frail and had a fall and couldn't come this year. I wasn't surprised. I knew she would always return to Terceira if she was able.

"But John was here," he said. "He was the king at Sanjoaninas."

I was right. I had known that teenager on the float.

When I reached John by phone, we spoke of many things. His family had moved from Boston to Florida, and that was why I hadn't been able to find him. But the part that whipped me right back to summer days at the Biscoitos pools watching his aimless splashing was when he told me he was on the swim team.

A Misguided Search

Mannie was walking down Serreta's main street as I was coming from the other direction.

In Terceira, people hardly ever left it at a nodded hello. They draped over lava-rock walls, sat on church steps, and halted their cars for a chat. Gabbing was a key activity. At the spot where our paths crossed, we sat down on a wall overlooking the ocean. It just so happened that it belonged to the house where Mannie had grown up.

"This very house?" I asked.

"Yes," said Mannie. "I remember sitting right here and it looking like the ocean was on fire when the volcano exploded on Faial."

Mannie was a child when Capelinhos erupted and gave his family a way to emigrate. He left for America when he was ten.

There is something magic about being ten years old. You're still a little kid, with all the elasticity and glee of childhood, but you're old enough to be defined. Immigrating at that age, Mannie never felt that he didn't quite belong in either place, which was common with older immigrants.

"I always felt one hundred percent Azorean and one hundred percent American," he said. "At school I was one, at home another. I liked it that way. I still like being more than one thing."

Still, there was hardship. His father, the family's sole breadwinner, worked on a dairy like most Azorean immigrants to California. He was seriously injured on the job. Mannie remembers the two dairy owners whispering outside his father's hospital door before coming in with their offer. They said they couldn't afford to hold his job. They would have to hire someone else—unless there was another solution.

"That boy of yours there—he's pretty big. We could change around chores, and he could work before and after school until you're back," one of them said.

For close to a year, Mannie got up before dawn and went to bed after dark, putting in hard physical labor. Any hours he wasn't in school, he was working on the dairy. He never told his schoolmates about his other life. He remembers falling asleep anytime he sat still. He was eleven.

"You have to realize that to them, they were being kind," Mannie said. "What would have happened to us if my dad lost his job?"

I asked him about Maria Elvita—I was still hoping she'd just bump into her suitor from her youth. He said it was her last week on Terceira. I couldn't believe it. She'd been here for a six-week stay. How could one summer possibly go so fast?

We all met again for dinner at Ti Choa's.

I asked Maria Elvita whether she had talked to Arturo. She looked sad when she said she hadn't seen him.

That does it, I thought. *I'm going to find him.*

The next morning I was in Barney early, giving my daily please-start prayer. Maria Elvita's plane was leaving the next day.

I figured I would begin with Chef. He could ask the members of Ti-Notas. Like most musicians, they had day jobs, and between them, they were in cows, biology, nursing, teaching, and public service, so I would have inquiries in many worlds.

When I got to the fire station, Chef came out rubbing his eyes after a busy night shift of people getting drunk and hurt at festas. I'd mentioned Arturo to him before, including that I'd heard he might have come back to Terceira and become a policeman.

Chef made one call. On his end of the line I heard, *"Pronto, pronto, pronto"*—"OK, OK, OK." When he got off the phone, he asked for my notebook and pen and drew a map. He tapped at a point in Biscoitos. "That's his weekend house," he said.

It was Saturday.

I called Maria Elvita. She didn't answer. I left a message telling her to call me right back—that I had Arturo's address. I went to the market to kill time and pick up groceries. Still no return call from Maria Elvita, and she wasn't picking up her phone. The day was ticking away.

I called Mannie and Mary, excited to have my quarry located.

"Maybe she's not answering her phone because she knows it's a bad idea," Mannie said.

It was a pretty day. The house was near the port. I drove that way, telling myself I was just going to look at the sea.

I pulled over to spy on a lush yard with neatly trimmed hedges. A man was in the garden, inspecting his plants.

I sat frozen in my car and did not approach him. At first I told myself it was because he might not speak English. But then I realized it was because Mannie was right. It was none of my business, and it was a bad idea. If Maria Elvita got on the plane tomorrow without speaking to the man she loved when she was seventeen, that was fine. It's not just endings that matter.

Good Night, Good Friends

I may have known him fifteen years, but I had never before seen the Jack Moody who arrived in the Azores. Fresh haircut, crisp white shirt, nice leather jacket. The Moody I knew was forever outfitted in fleece. Or an ancient San Francisco Giants hoodie. He smiled at my gaping and winked.

"I told you I wanted to try," he said.

We went to Ti Choa and over dinner tried to pin down when or how we had come to this point. He said it might have been the first time he saw my legs when I was wearing yoga pants while we were making dinner. I found this a ridiculous candidate for a turning point because I was a writer who worked at home, so he had been seeing my legs in yoga pants for about a decade. On the other hand, he must have always had eyes. But I'd never before noticed how they changed color.

I thought about Romana's pumpkins: sometimes life is better with mystery.

We left Terceira for São Jorge and the *fajã* I had sized up earlier as a romantic getaway. We had planned on four days but were now on our second week. We had flexibility because when weighing whether Moody should come over, I had relied on a standby of decision-making: What's the worst that could happen?

The worst, as I had imagined it, would be things not going well and our being awkwardly stuck together until his departure date. I had suggested a one-way ticket so we could get him on a plane in a hurry if need be.

Instead, the availability on our first rental cottage ran out, and we had just arrived at our second place. In this little seashell of a village, it meant moving one bump of a hill over—the streets were too meandering to estimate it in blocks. Luísa, who rented out the house for her brother, who lived in California, came over to welcome us along with her husband, two young sons, and two nieces. Her husband brought a bottle of homemade wine. He didn't speak English, but hand signals are fine for pouring a glass and raising a toast. The kids were playing soccer with Murphy, no language required. The nine-year-old son told me it was "Good Night, Good Friends" night.

I didn't know what that meant.

To demonstrate, the eight of them gathered close and with their beatific faces and voices sang us a song.

I still did not know what it meant.

That night we went to bed about midnight, which I considered quite early and Moody considered late. In the distance, I could hear people singing. Soon the troupe was on our street bellowing out songs. In Terceira it had been marching bands at every turn; here it seemed to be carolers.

I asked Moody whether he wasn't vastly amused.

He sleepily said he wouldn't go as far as vastly.

The singing got even closer. I heard someone shout, "*Americanos*—no sleeping!" There was a loud knock.

I threw on jeans and a T-shirt and went to open the door. On the step were about thirty people, including Albertina's older brother, Duarte, who was here for his yearly stay in the family home.

"We are going to sing for you," said Duarte.

Moody came out with rumpled hair and flip-flops and sat beside me as they launched into a rousing song—a few of them with remarkable voices and all of them with passion. I was handed a glass of wine.

The crowd sang another ditty that ended with "drink, drink, drink" (in Portuguese, but some things are just clear). I raised a glass and drank up. Moody got the same treatment.

Duarte said we must now come along with them to other houses, where the crowd would sing to the owners, who would take a drink and join the procession until the whole village was carousing together. He said it was an old tradition that went back to when everyone made their own wine and went house to house to taste one another's vintages.

I had never heard of this custom before, and it made me wonder whether it was unique to this one island. "Is it all of Azores or just São Jorge?" I asked Duarte.

He seemed shocked.

"Only here. This *fajã*. Not the *whole* island," he said.

Silly me. There are eight thousand people on São Jorge. Did I think they would all keep the same standard traditions?

Luísa had known we wouldn't have goodies ready, so she'd brought over snacks and wine for the communal stop at our place. She and her husband were carrying things back to their house next door. Duarte noticed they were headed home.

"You must come for the procession!" he cried.

They said they had the children. The crowd was having none of it. The husband put the youngest on his back, and off we all went. They left the door to their house wide-open.

The moon was out, and light sparkled on the ocean. The white houses with their red-tile roofs and the church steeple and the soft hills glowed. The little port with its couple of old fishing boats seemed lit from beneath. No one carried a flashlight or needed to.

One man, Joe, led the way, carrying a stick flying a Portuguese flag, a piece of dried fish, and various vegetables. He said it symbolized something but he'd forgotten what.

At each house we were introduced with much cheek kissing to our hosts. Most of them split their lives between here, where their families came from, and California. One was a goat farmer in Lemoore, another a businessman in Tracy. There were couples from Turlock, Hilmar, and Merced. With the two of us recently escaped Fresnans, you had the whole Central Valley. At each house there was a table full of cookies, chips, sausages, and, of course, São Jorge cheese—the island's major economic engine and favorite snack.

And booze. Lots of it.

Before I got the hang of hiding and dodging from proffered glasses, I politely drank *aguardente*. It could be up to 60 percent alcohol. I was pretty sure the two glasses I drank were in the upper limit, judging by my lack of sobriety. At the oldest house in the village—a century-old cottage up a steep hill—Moody shot a glass of whiskey almost as ancient as the house and the man who lived there. I wouldn't say the entire village was drunk, but I do recall Duarte—who is a respected Stanford educator—grabbing my hand and giggling wildly as we sprinted up a hill and to the next stop.

Murphy had been tagging along, trying to get a pat from each and every person, but somewhere along the way I lost track of him. I wasn't worried. The village was so small and traffic-free that in the mornings we just opened the door and let Murphy run down to the port for a swim. We could hear him yipping as he did his laps, and he showed up later wet and hungry. Tonight, he must have gone for a dip.

At each house there was more singing. Duarte said the song had endless verses and translated a few about a man telling his wife he spent only little bits of money on wine and the woman telling her husband he was spending their fortune in little bits. The chorus was, "Before I make it to those pearly gates, bury me in a wine barrel."

At the final house, Luísa came in at the tail end of the crowd and began telling a story that had people doubled over with laughter. My ears picked out the word *cão*. I was immediately on alert. I grabbed Duarte and dragged him over to translate for me.

He said Luísa was explaining that they had left in a hurry to join the procession and had not put away the treats they had laid out for the stop at their house. I knew just enough Portuguese to translate for myself the list of things Murphy had eaten. Luísa's hand gestures filled me in on serving sizes.

- *O grande bolo*—one super big, big cake
- *Biscoitos*—a plate of cookies
- *Batata fritas*—a huge bowl of potato chips
- *Cerveja*—a puddle where they had emptied opened bottles of leftover warm beer

I was mortified. Everyone else was laughing.

Luísa's husband said in Portuguese and Duarte translated, "Murphy is going to feel like the rest of us in the morning."

An Idyll

I looked up the word *idyll*.

"An extremely happy, peaceful, or picturesque period or situation, typically an idealized or unsustainable one," according to *Oxford*. Too bad about that last bit, but it did seem to be the word I was looking for.

We were still on São Jorge, and the days had fallen into a sameness that I didn't mind. After a late breakfast, Moody, Murphy, and I went for a walk. The footpath that skirted the cliffs and dropped to the sea, or the road that went by the church and along the sea, or the road in front of our house that took us straight to the sea.

Every day, Moody and Murphy swam in the spectacular ocean pools protected by lava rock a short hike from the port. I went in the water some days but chickened out on others. It wasn't the ocean that scared me—it was the climb down the long ladder. I've always had a thing about heights. I was the kid who had to hold her grandmother's hand while walking on top of the semitruck tires that my neighborhood considered playground equipment. I didn't confess this to Moody. I kept forgetting that he was no longer my cranky hiking partner who would harrumph at such a thing. Even using the ladder put me in the circle of the nondaring. There were other people diving from high, craggy spires. It was such a long way down that their bodies seemed stamped on the blue sky for impossibly frozen amounts of time.

We walked home to make lunch and then lazed on the shaded terrace, reading books or chatting.

Moody told me about the time he was traveling with his buddy Joe and they met a guy named Charlie Khan in Germany. Charlie gave them his family's address in Peshawar. They arrived unannounced in Pakistan just in time to go to a bachelor party with Charlie's brothers, Jabbar and Babar.

As he told his story, I found myself getting a little mad.

Moody had held out on me for so many years. I thought of one particularly dreary Christmas Eve. We'd worked a newspaper shift together, then gone to get Chinese food because we were both alone with no plans. I'd painfully tried to get a conversation going while we ate greasy noodles under depressing fluorescent lights. Note the *painfully*. Why didn't he tell me then about Jabbar and Babar or Mr. Artale, the first man with a tattoo to move into Moody's childhood neighborhood? Moody was seven at the time, and the tattoo was of a woman with a sailor's cap and bare breasts. "It was astonishing," he told me.

But I kept my annoyance to myself. Things seemed pretty perfect—best to not ruin it with a "How dare you used to be boring!"

In the evenings, we went out to dinner. There was never any tiresome "Where do you want to go?" conversation. There was only one restaurant for miles. It was a short walk—down by the sea, of course.

The beginning of the *fajã*'s yearly festa was first signaled by big vats of grapes in front of the church, ready to be stomped. At the restaurant, I looked at a list of the activities and asked the waitress what a cow fight was.

"It's a bullfight but with lady cows," she said.

It was our afternoon plan unless I first heard from Donald Mota. The night before, I had gotten an email from Donald, an Azorean Californian. I had first met him when I'd written the story about California *forçados*, the bullfighters who line up like dominoes and let the bull plow into them. Donald said it was a way for him to stay connected to his Azorean heritage. He had told me it was his father who first took him to the bullfights, where older Azoreans called him Donald-Son-of-Mota.

When his father was dying of lung cancer, Donald found escape in being a *forçado*. He would hear his heart pound in his ears and feel a rush with each breath while he waited for the bull.

He was in São Jorge on a short trip visiting family. For years we'd talked about crossing paths in the Azores, but both of us kept planning trips that never happened. I wrote him right back. I didn't get an answer. We were finally both on the same island, but we might miss each other.

When Moody and I got to the field where they were having the party, we were greeted warmly by most everyone as if we were old friends. I considered this proof of my Second-Day-of-Dance-Class Theory.

The Second-Day-of-Dance-Class Theory

When I taught dance, often on a child's first day at class, she (it was almost always a she) would cry and wouldn't hold hands with the other little girls.

The next week she would be all smiles and even know our foot-in, foot-out curtsy goodbye dance. Her mystified parents would tell me how she had practiced all week.

Later, reporting in insular small towns, a photographer and I would go around introducing ourselves and get a stilted, standoffish reception. We'd show up a couple of days later, and faces would light up in friendly recognition—"Hey! You're those reporters. How ya doing?"

Thus, the Second-Day-of-Dance-Class Theory (alternatively known as the One-Trip-Is-Not-Enough School of Reporting) holds that when traveling, one should forget constant exploration. Go back to the same spots. You'll be recognized as a familiar face and you'll discover more.

All the people we recognized from taking the same daily walks and making the same daily stops were sitting or leaning on the rough stone walls that circled the field.

There were four wooden crates, far smaller than the crates at a bullfight, in a grassy field. The hills all around were dotted with black-and-white cows, making me wonder why they would truck in more cows.

My phone rang. It was Donald Mota. He said he had just arrived with his family at a bullfight and wondered whether we would we like to meet him there. I said sure and asked what town. He named the village right up the hill.

"I think they meant a cow fight," I said, scanning the crowd.

Sure enough, there he was, over by the beer tent. I was happy to see him and surprised to recognize him. He had cropped the long curly hair I thought of as his trademark.

As a *forçado* he was the *rabejador*—the last guy in line. After the bull hit and slowed to a stop under a mound of bullfighters, the *rabejador* grabbed the tail, and the bull chased him in circles while the crowd roared. Donald always added extra flair by throwing one hand in the air as his feet kicked up dust and his wild curly hair flapped.

Having watched him do that, I figured he was going to be the first over the wall to wrestle with a cow.

"No way. These free-for-alls make me nervous. There's no control. Anything can happen," he said. "Besides, cows can be really mean."

They let out the first cow, small and black. It was the female version of one of the bred-to-be-aggressive bulls. This was no mellow, grass-nibbling milk cow.

A dozen people were in the field, but this cow zeroed in on just one, a lanky guy wearing a tweed cap and chartreuse-striped Nike trainers. The cow chased him all the way across the field. She was right on his heels. He jumped on a ramp leading to all of us behind the wall. Her horns were still right at his heels. Mr. Chartreuse-Swoosh rolled off the ramp and ducked behind a truck's cab. The second he was out of sight, the cow turned around.

Donald said the folk wisdom held that unlike bulls, which could be easily distracted, cows took mental snapshots of one person and would zero in on a target as if they had radar. "You don't want to catch a cow's eyes," he said.

The spectacle inspired Moody to reclaim the photojournalist in him. He was up on walls, crouching here and there, wielding a smartphone like a paintbrush. Later, I laughed at his favorite shot. In the foreground was the cow, just a whisper from Chartreuse-Swoosh. Along the wall was a line of faces in every mode of rapt attention. Some with their hands to their chest, some with hands to their mouth, some laughing, others with eyes bugged out and mouths agape.

Another cow. The same scene. She picked one skinny guy and ignored all others. He ran the entire field, a cigarette dangling from his lips. The cow was so close as he leaped the wall that he grabbed her horn for a push.

"Damn," said Donald. "You don't want to mess with a cow."

His shorter hair showed off his chiseled face. Good looks ran in the Mota family. Which reminded me of the last time I'd seen Donald in California.

In Turlock, there is a gas station that used to sell hats that read, "Turlock—Known for Absolutely Nothing." Turlock is next to even-smaller Hilmar, where there are a lot of Portuguese saints painted on house tiles because it's one of the towns with the highest percentage of Azorean residents in the United States.

I had visited Donald on a ranch outside Hilmar down streets with no names—just numbers. Donald and his friends were having a bullfight practice, and I showed up to look for someone who was going to the Azores for the summer. It was for a newspaper article I was writing.

A man sitting on a hay bale near mine said, "You should talk to my daughter. She's considering going back for the first time, and she's very famous on the internet." He was named Tony—as are many men in Hilmar and the Azores. I had already noticed him because he was tall and handsome and wearing the wrong cowboy boots. These weren't I-know-my-way-around-a-dairy boots; these were I-weekend-at-a-winery boots.

I was pretty sure if an Azorean daughter was famous on the internet for something her dad would mention, she must sing fado, the Portuguese art of the sad song. If a girl could sing fado, she would be a Hilmar YouTube sensation. Why, she might have hundreds of followers.

"What's she famous for?" I asked knowingly.

"She's an internationally acclaimed fashion blogger," he said.

Did I mention I was sitting on a hay bale?

"If you're planning verticals for brand building, we might consider letting you talk to Bethany, but we absolutely would not sell the rights to video," he told me. "What's this for?"

"It's for a newspaper," I said.

"Print! Oh-ho-ho," he laughed. "If your editors even knew you were talking to me, they would be peeing their pants."

When feeling threatened, a person can puff up in the manner of a defenseless fish trying to fool predators. I squared my shoulders. I stood tall.

"I think my editors can retain control of their bladders at the mention of a fashion blogger. My editors deal with world leaders every day," I told him.

"Oh!" he said. "Bethany just interviewed the president."

He held out his phone with a photo of his pretty daughter, Bethany Mota, two other YouTube stars—one known for green lipstick—and then President Barack Obama.

Puffer fish, by the way, are a threatened species.

I sneaked out to my car and looked up Donald's niece Bethany Mota on my phone. She was beautiful, with the wide eyes of a woodland creature. She had 1.2 million Twitter followers, 2.3 million

Instagram followers, and 5.1 million YouTube subscribers. She had made it to the finals on *Dancing with the Stars.* One headline read, "From Bethany Mota to Kim Jong-Un—Ten of the World's Most Influential Millennials."

Her fame began with haul videos. She would go shopping and pull her purchases—glitter nail polish, lace-print jeans, scented candles—out of bags, squealing, "Guys! Guys! Look!" as a webcam rolled. Hers was the delight of a million children on Christmas morning.

Her father told me Bethany had started making the videos after she was bullied at school. Now she was especially revered by young women in Japan, some of the legions who counted themselves as Mota-vators and showed up in the thousands to meet the high priestess of plucky shopaholics.

Stay

Moody and I were at dinner, chatting about pirates because there used to be a lot of them in the Azores. I wanted to ditch the medieval history lesson and talk about us. We didn't live in the same part of California any longer. He'd moved to a tiny town up north to be close to his kids, who worked at their mother's country store. There had been no further declarations of intentions.

"So," I said, with no finesse at all. "What would a happy relationship look like to you?"

He blanched. Exactly the way he had years ago. His ability to immediately lose color was astonishing.

He stammered and stuttered something about did I want to talk about us, and then *he broke out into a sweat.*

I'm not exaggerating. He even pointed it out. "Look, there are drops of sweat on my forehead," he said.

Something inside me shut down. I could almost hear doors slamming in my head.

"Momentary lapse," I said with a smile. "Calm down, and I'll tell you more pirate stories."

That night, I stayed up late and hugged my dog, long after Moody had gone to bed.

The next morning, I stumbled out to the kitchen. Moody had the table set with a colorful tablecloth, bowls of cut-up fruit, breads, yogurt, and toppings. He handed me a freshly brewed cup of coffee. I sipped and thought in a just-woke-up muzzy way, *Oh well, there are worse things than a just-summer romance.* We were all adults here. I could do jaded.

But suddenly Moody was a torrent of words.

"Do-you-think-we're-not-suited? I-was-thinking-about-it-all-last-night. But-I-think-things-are-going-well. Do-you-think-maybe-you're-just-looking-for-problems? But-if-you're-still-hung-up-on-someone-else . . ."

I. Am. *Not.* A. Morning. Person.

Seriously, it is hard for me to form sentences in the morning, much less analyze a relationship.

"Of course I think we're unsuited," I blurted out. "That's what makes it interesting."

"Interesting?" Moody asked. "OK, I'll take interesting for now."

We walked the long way around to the ocean pools, stopping to watch the waves and a fisherman picking his way over rocks carrying a pole three times the length of his body. We made plans to return to Terceira but didn't mention anything about our return to California.

Back in Terceira, the corn had grown tall. The lavender and pink pom-poms of hydrangeas had given way to hillsides of spiky yellow flowers with red antennae. You could snap off the end and drink the sugar water inside. They had at least three different Azorean names—a throwback to the days when few people had cars and there was different vocabulary even between villages that were a few miles apart. Their English name was kahili ginger.

One afternoon we set out for a drive and found the road around the island lined with throngs of pilgrims walking to Serreta. Delcione had told me that she remembered the faithful walking barefoot when she was a girl. For some, even that wasn't enough sacrifice. Del was haunted by the memory of an old woman wrapped in shawls crawling on her hands and knees to the church with bloody palms. This crowd wore sports clothes. Lots of bright pink and running shoes. Even older men with walking sticks and Portuguese caps finished their look with yellow fluorescent safety vests.

It was one of those island days when the sun was shining but white clouds were moving so fast across the blue sky that you knew change was coming and you had to sit in the sun while you could.

Moody and I went to Ti Choa's, chose a table on the little patio, and ordered gin and tonics. In Portugal, these are concoctions with the garnish—different combinations of cucumber, orange, lime, juniper berries—matched to the type of gin. Before Sergio was a waiter at Ti Choa's, he worked at a fancy restaurant in Angra where he said he'd had to dress like one of those "black-and-white birds who live on ice." He had recently added his cocktail expertise from his previous job to Ti Choa's otherwise traditional menu.

Sergio spoke English with a slight British accent and a continuous sad sigh. His words were always kind and helpful but delivered in a tone of regret. All summer, the forever deadpan Sergio had been saying he was looking forward to the vacation he'd have when the restaurant closed for the festa so he could sleep the whole time.

Now, he said with an exaggerated sigh, a friend had called him and told him he had to walk with her on her pilgrimage.

I said it was an awfully big crowd and that I had been under the impression that the pilgrimage was for those who had been granted a miracle.

"Yes," Sergio said. "But isn't that everyone?"

Festa season ended. I could drive around the island without running into a single roadblock set up for a bullfight in the street. Every week there were more closed-up houses as the immigrants returned home—or was it as the emigrants left home? Just as in California in the fall, the days got warmer and the sky bluer after tourist season. Call it the back-to-school curse.

One day, I sat in the window trying very hard to memorize the patterns the sun made on the Azorean ocean.

Moody came over and looked out the window with me.

"You should stay," he said. "You're not ready to go back."

I had budgeted only to September. I had driven cross-country from California so Murphy wouldn't have to be in the belly of a plane for seven hours and left my car at a friend's house in Maine. I told Moody it wouldn't be practical to stay into winter, but even as I protested, his idea started tap-dancing in my mind: "Stay, stay, stay."

"You've never been practical and you've always been broke," Moody said. "Why mess with what's working for you?"

He had to get back. He had plane tickets for a trip with his brother and he wanted to see his kids. I still had five months before I had to be back at work from a one-year leave. I watched him pack.

At the cozy airport we joked about how he would get to eat Mexican food and Thai food in California, while it was more grilled fish and boiled potatoes for me.

When they called his flight, he shoved a paper in my hand, saying, "Here, hold this."

He kissed me goodbye and said, "Take care, Marcum."

"I'll miss you, Moody," I told him. We had never lost the newsroom habit of last names.

I walked all the way back to the car before I noticed I was still holding the folded piece of paper he'd handed to me.

I opened it.

"There's more ahead of us," he had written. "I may just have to come back. I'll see you soon, whether it's in California or Azores. *Beijos.*" He'd signed it *Jack* but crossed that out and written *Moody*.

I waved his note at Murphy in the back seat. Note: A lot of people talk to their dogs. It's not just me.

"Look at that," I said. "*Beijos*—he's picking up the lingo. And maybe he'll come back."

Moody had said he had lost his passion for taking photos. But in California he picked up his cameras. He sent me photos of butter-gold fields. Drops suspended on bark that has been bone dry. Condensation on windows. Puddles reflecting mountains.

Rain.

Cagarros

I wasn't the only one who had stayed longer than expected. The cagarros were still on Terceira too. By this time, the baby seabirds should have left their nests. It was almost November, and few had been spotted on the island.

It might mean good news: Perhaps they had made it to sea safely. One of the reasons the cagarros were threatened was that the young kept getting lost on their first flight out to sea.

No one was exactly sure why. One theory was that the birds traveled by moonlight and starlight and the modern world's artificial lights confused them. Other scientists thought it could be electromagnetic fields that were scrambling the bird's navigation systems. So now, if they weren't ending up on the roadway, where they could get hit by cars or chased by dogs and cats, then they might be safely flying over the water, where they belonged.

Another possibility was that perhaps few birds had been born this year. Maybe predators got the eggs. Maybe the adult cagarros didn't reproduce. If that was the case, it would be devastating for the survival of the species.

Helder, the lead singer of Ti-Notas, was a biologist working with a public campaign to save cagarros. He was going out to look for nests. I was going with him.

We started our hike between Serreta and the village of Raminho along the sea cliffs. Morning glories covered the ground and trees. The vines' huge purple flowers cascaded over branches like waterfalls and piled up in mounds along the trail. Helder shook his head at the takeover by an invasive species. I thought it looked like a fairy tale.

The sky was a gauzy gray, the ocean a bright, silken turquoise. The hills looked greener than ever before—but I thought that on most days. These were all things that made me not yet ready to leave the island. The entrance to the trail leading down the cliffs wasn't marked, and it was generous to call it a trail. Once again I internally noted that I was afraid of heights. It was quite inconvenient at times like this.

The name of the hidden trail was Tavares. According to folklore, it was the name of a man who had lived in Serreta long ago. He was a hermit, seldom speaking to neighbors. He didn't go to Sunday services, which in his time period, in this place, was considered very strange. He owned a lot of books, and he could be seen reading them by candlelight, which made the villagers surmise he was an educated man—perhaps a priest gone astray. But on some days he would dress up and wear a suit pinned with medals, so maybe he had been a military man.

One day, Tavares had a vision. Our Lady Mary of Serreta, the one to whom people made a pilgrimage each year, appeared to him. She said there was rumbling beneath the sea. She told him that unless he repented and started praying, a volcano would erupt and kill everyone.

People started seeing him in fields on his knees, praying. His clothes became torn and dirty, and he went from being the village hermit to the village madman. He told everyone he had to keep praying or there would be a great loss of life.

He was wandering in the very area where I was now walking—big boulders loomed over the narrow trail—when a rock crashed down into his skull. He made it to town with the rock still embedded in his head. And he died.

Two days later, a volcano beneath the sea erupted. The 1867 submarine eruption is well documented. It was close to the island and set off earthquakes so strong that they changed the landscape. The earth pushed into new hills and opened up in deep ravines. But everyone survived. The legend has it that the hermit's death broke the protection holding the volcano back but that his prayers had saved the people.

Those earthquakes haven't been forgotten. Every spring there is still a procession from Raminho. The crowd carries icons from the Holy Spirit festivals and from traditional Catholicism. At spots where the earthquake from 150 years ago caused the most upheaval, people drop to their knees and sing a song at least as old as those quakes. Helder, who sings as easily and often as most people laugh, sang part of the song as we hiked. I couldn't understand the words. It was the melody that got to me, mournful mixed with quiet joy.

"I get chills when I sing it," Helder said.

He remembered going on the procession as a boy. It always started before first light.

"It feels weird," Helder said. "Dawn comes, and everyone kneels and sings a song accepting that this ancient thing happened and could happen again. When I was a boy, it scared me."

As an adult, he found it inspiring.

"I'm an environmental educator. I warn that the natural world has to be respected," he said. "When I go down on my knees and sing that song, the feeling is—I don't know the English word for it—it's like I'm outside myself and connected to other times and so aware of all the beauty and all the threat."

"Yeah," I said. "I don't know the English word for that either."

But I knew the feeling.

During the Rim Fire in California, a huge pyrocumulus cloud formed every afternoon. People in Groveland, a little (by California standards) town of six hundred, came out and stood in front of their clapboard houses and potted geraniums and watched as the firecloud grew higher than the Sierra Nevada. I would stand there awed, and without words I deeply understood that if it didn't rain, the next fires could be even bigger, and if the rains did come and they were too hard or too much, those burned hillsides would wash away in floods. It was all so precarious—right on the edge of cataclysmic. But nearby were flowers in flower boxes and pines that had not burned and a lost dog that had returned home and a restaurant opening for dinner, and you could feel everyone in the street breathing sighs of gratitude that it was all still here. If even for just a little longer.

That's what Helder's song sounded like.

He slowed his steps. We were in an area of rock outcrops between tall *vassoura* bushes. The nests should be found in the nooks in rocks. Helder pointed to a few telltale feathers. He crouched down low to peer into a crevice, then waved me over. It was dark between the rocks, so it took a second for me to make out that the white at the bottom was a tail feather and that the cotton puff was a bird's body. I could see a small, curved yellow beak and, oh look, two bright eyes looking right into mine.

"He's perfect," Helder said. "Ready to fly."

Helder's job included taking kids on hikes and explaining the cagarros' nesting habits, which research had revealed over only the past few decades. He confessed that for his young audiences, he broke scientific protocol and asked the kids to think of a baby cagarro in terms of how they would feel in the same situation.

"I need to make them care, or cagarros will disappear," he said. "They can get the more grown-up version later."

He told them how adult cagarros returned each year to the same nest, the same mate. Each couple had one egg. He told them the mom and dad took turns swooping over the ocean to get food and sitting on the nest. Come fall, the parents left. The baby stayed in the nest a few weeks longer, getting all its feathers. Then the baby felt the open sea calling. With no lessons, all by itself, the fledgling walked out to the cliff and—with something deep inside saying it could do it—flew. Hopefully far out on the ocean where it met up with others of its kind.

In 1995, the Azores regional government launched an SOS campaign to save the birds. Each fall, schoolchildren are given cagarros information packets. Posters, radio, and television remind people to be on the lookout for lost baby birds. Fire stations and police stations are drop-off points, and volunteers pick up the recovered birds and release them at sea.

The cagarros had seemed to be heading for extinction, but now their raucous, crazy love songs would be part of the future.

Most of the cagarros story I knew before. On my first trip, when I was so desperate to return, I had taken them as my personal token. I was going to be like the cagarros, I told myself—I'd be back next year.

Helder found another nook, and we saw another baby cagarro. I started looking on my own and found two nests. Then another. The fledglings were here. They just weren't yet ready to leave.

Onstage at Ti-Notas concerts, Helder had an infectious spirit. He would throw his arms to the sky, spin around, and hold a microphone out to the crowd that he had singing along. But I had never seen him look as joyous as he did on our return hike that day. He kept shaking his head and laughing to himself. We had found more baby cagarros than he expected.

A few weeks later, I was walking Murphy on a sidewalk in Biscoitos. The path, set apart by a low wall, followed along the ocean. Murphy suddenly yanked on his leash and tried to jump the short wall. I figured he had found an ice cream wrapper. He started barking. I peeked over the wall.

Wedged into a corner was a young cagarro. It had all its feathers, which were the same gray and white as the wall. If it hadn't been for Murphy, I would have never seen it.

I didn't know what to do. I had no box, and I had an overly excited Labrador retriever.

I called Chef, who lived one village over. I caught him on his one day off, while he was building a chicken coop. He said he was surprised he had heard the phone ring over his hammering. He had a box in his car in case he ever spotted a lost baby bird. He'd be right over.

When he got there, he said I should pick the bird up, since I'd never done it before. He held Murphy and talked me through taking off my raincoat and using it as a blanket. I tossed it over the cagarro and grabbed the bird behind the neck. The little cagarro loudly protested, sticking out a long, pink tongue as he screeched. We got him into the box, complete with breathing holes and stamped with "*Governo do Açores S.O.S. Cagarro.*"

I was exhilarated—more excited than I would have thought I'd feel over one little bird.

"But it's more than that," Chef said. "The cagarros were almost lost forever, and everyone worked together to save them. Isn't it an amazing feeling?" he asked. "Every time I rescue a cagarro, it is everything. It is Azores."

I remembered how Chef had laughed during my low point at the end of my last trip. "Here's to nothing," he had toasted in the face of my litany of no job, no money, no love. He had said he knew I'd be back, just like a cagarro.

Now, years later, he was explaining that he'd take the bird I had found back to the fire station. Volunteers would put a band on its leg, and when the bird returned to nest next year, I would receive an email.

I told him that part of what he said was wrong. I knew this because of something Helder had taught me on the hike: the first time cagarros left, they were gone seven years before their first return.

Chef's head snapped back.

"How long were you gone before you came back?" he asked sharply.

I grinned. "Seven years," I said. I nodded at the box holding the cagarro.

Tomorrow, someone would pick it up, drive it to the edge of a cliff, open the box, pick up the cagarro, and toss the bird into the air so it could fly out to sea.

"Hey," I said. "Here's to everything."

CODA

My Tenth Island (a list in the making)

High Sierra lakes.
Turquoise sea.
Giant sequoias dropping clumps of snow.
The scent of creosote in the desert after the first rain.
Sunshine.
Family.
Friends who become family.
Chuva.
Always, always, always an island across the way.

ACKNOWLEDGMENTS

First and foremost, thank you to those who shared their stories and their time and who populate this book.

I don't even know the names of those first patrons who sent an unknown writer to the Azores. But thank you. I hope this book finds you and that you know you had something to do with it.

Thanks to the two Bs: Bonnie Nadell, my ever-insightful agent, and to Little A's Barry Harbaugh, who believed in the book and bought it. And to editor Laura Van der Veer, who shepherded the manuscript through production with carefulness and cheer, and the rest of the team at Little A.

Thanks to Kari Howard, my friend and longtime editor on newspaper stories, who shaped the early drafts and was right about everything. We are a team. She's the brilliant half.

Thanks to Brynn Callahan, hired for typing, but valued for her quirky intellect and heartfelt feedback. Thanks to my fellow Nieman Fellows Dustin Dwyer, João Pina, Lisa Lerer, and historian Rachel Nolan for early reads and whip-smart suggestions.

Thanks to Teofilo Cota for showing me the Azores through his eyes. To the Costa family for making me feel at home in Turlock and Terceira. To Frank and Bernadette Coelho for loaning a stranger the family home.

Thank you to Barbara "Taz" Anderson for being there every step of the way—with margaritas when needed. Thanks to the Hamayelians for giving an *odar* a family and to them and the rest of my friends for being good sports about being turned into book characters.

Last, but in no way least, thanks to Mark Crosse, my Jack Moody, here properly identified, who added a happy ending to the book—and my life—and made me pancakes when I was on deadline.

ABOUT THE AUTHOR

Photo © Mark Crosse

Diana Marcum is a narrative writer for the *Los Angeles Times*. In 2015, she won the Pulitzer Prize for feature writing for her newspaper portraits of farmers, field-workers, and others in the drought-stricken towns of California's Central Valley.